Growing in God's Love

Every Story, Every Lesson—
All in One Powerful Collection

Help nurture the faith of the children in your life with *Growing in God's Love: A Story Bible*. This engaging resource features 150 popular Bible stories that are organized by thirteen themes, including "Strong Women and Men," "Listening for God," "Parables," "Healings and Miracles," and more. *Growing in God's Love* features diverse artwork from more than twenty artists to appeal to a variety of ages and learning styles. Three reflection questions—Hear, See, Act—are included at the end of each story to help children further ponder the message of the story.

Designed to spark curiosity and deepen faith, *Growing in God's Love: A Story Bible Curriculum* brings the stories of the Bible to life for children ages 5–10. This engaging, multiage curriculum is a companion to the best-selling *Growing in God's Love: A Story Bible* and offers 148 lesson plans organized into thirty-five thoughtfully crafted units.

"This is the kind of devotional families can grow with—not recover from. *Growing in God's Love: A Family Devotional* is expansive, inclusive, and deeply rooted in a faith that makes space for curiosity, justice, and wonder. The stories center on voices often left out—women who resist, chosen families, people wrestling with what's fair. Each devotion invites children (and their grown-ups) to reflect on what it means to live as God's people today. With language that honors all kinds of families and questions that invite action, this devotional is a gift for anyone raising children with a faith that liberates rather than confines."

—Daneen Akers, author of *Holy Troublemakers & Unconventional Saints* and *Dear Mama God*

"*Growing in God's Love: A Family Devotional* is exactly the kind of resource families have been asking me about for years. It is grounded, imaginative, and wonderfully easy to use. With accessible reflections and thoughtful invitations to engage, this devotional draws families into Scripture and faith practice in a way that is both meaningful and sustainable. It is a resource families will return to again and again on their journey of faith. What a treasure!"

—Traci Smith, author of *Faithful Families: Creating Sacred Moments at Home* and director of Family Faith Every Day

"I love this book! As a parent whose faith has deconstructed and evolved, I believe *Growing in God's Love: A Family Devotional* is a godsend. It is hopeful, reflective, and truly safe for the whole family to enjoy together. Each reading offers parents an easy way to start important conversations, inspire hope and kindness, and add a little 'good news' to everyday life."

—Matthew Paul Turner, *New York Times* best-selling author of *What Is God Like?* and *When God Made You*

"At last! An inclusive, thought-provoking, well-written devotional that will be welcomed by progressive pastors and parents alike. *Growing in God's Love: A Family Devotional* invites readers on a journey through the Bible, offering fresh, thoughtful, relatable perspectives on its complex perennial tales."
—Glenys Nellist, award-winning author of *I Wonder: Exploring God's Grand Story* and the Love Letters from God series

"Talking to our children about faith, specifically Scripture, can be challenging. Many of the stories found in the Bible are not designed for children, and many of the ways we've been taught to interpret them only makes the process more difficult. That's why I am thrilled to recommend *Growing in God's Love: A Family Devotional*. While many devotionals are a dime a dozen, not this one. *Growing in God's Love* takes a careful, thoughtful approach to Scripture and does so while interpreting the Bible in better, more just, and generous ways. You won't regret making this resource part of your family's practice!"
—Josh Scott, pastor and author of *Cross-Examined: Reading the Bible in Times of Division* and *Parables: Putting Jesus's Stories in Their Place*

"Finally, a family devotion book that speaks to the *whole* family. Whether you're five, fifteen, or fifty-five, *Growing in God's Love* serves as a simple but gentle companion and guide on a lifelong journey. This is a book that will grow with families, setting the foundation for faithful conversation, active discipleship, and thoughtful engagement with God's Word active both in Scripture and in the world."
—Amy Lindeman Allen, Associate Professor of New Testament, Christian Theological Seminary, and author of *The Gifts They Bring: How Children in the Gospels Can Shape Inclusive Ministry*

"As a progressive pastor and parent, I'm constantly looking for resources that help families grow together in faith, deepen their understanding of God's love, and spark meaningful conversations across generations. *Growing in God's Love* is exactly that kind of resource. This beautifully crafted devotional offers accessible, thoughtful, and theologically grounded reflections that engage both children and adults. Its inclusive language, attention to diversity, and imaginative storytelling make it a breath of fresh air in the world of family devotionals. Each entry invites families into prayer, reflection, and action, fostering not only spiritual growth but also deeper connection with one another. I highly recommend *Growing in God's Love* to anyone seeking to nurture a household rooted in compassion, curiosity, and the transformative love of God."

—Caleb J. Lines, co-executive director of the Center for Progressive Christianity and author of *Awakened: A 52-Week Progressive Christian Devotional*

"I have recommended *Growing in God's Love: A Story Bible* to families and seminary students who will minister with families since it came out in 2019. *Growing in God's Love: A Family Devotional* is the perfect companion to the *Story Bible*. Like the *Story Bible*, it is accessible yet manages also to share the unfathomable depth of God's love and humans' relationship with God using Scripture as the road map. As families seek to incorporate their faith into practices at home, the accessibility, simplicity, and poignancy of *Growing in God's Love: A Family Devotional* will be a valuable asset. The devotions help young and old(er) alike to think deeply and welcome the Spirit into shaping our faith as we grow. The questions and activities help us connect in new and creative ways. There is no guilt, only the empowerment to practice faith across the generations at home. This devotional is a beautiful gift for Christian families."

—Emily A. Peck, Visiting Professor of Christian Formation and Young Adult Ministry, Wesley Theological Seminary, and author of *Arm in Arm with Adolescent Girls: Educating into the New Creation*

Growing in God's Love
A Family Devotional

Jessica Miller Kelley, Editor

© 2025 Westminster John Knox Press
Cover art copyright © 2025 Aimee Hagerty Johnson

First edition
Published by Westminster John Knox Press
Louisville, Kentucky

25 26 27 28 29 30 31 32 33 34—10 9 8 7 6 5 4 3 2 1

All rights reserved. No part of this book may be reproduced or transmitted in any form or by any means, electronic or mechanical, including photocopying, recording, or by any information storage or retrieval system, without permission in writing from the publisher. For information, address Westminster John Knox Press, 100 Witherspoon Street, Louisville, Kentucky 40202-1396. Or contact us online at www.wjkbooks.com.

Unless otherwise indicated, Scripture quotations are from the New Revised Standard Version Updated Edition. Copyright © 2021 National Council of Churches of Christ in the United States of America. Used by permission. All rights reserved worldwide.

Illustrations produced in partnership with Congregational Ministries Publishing of the Presbyterian Church (U.S.A.).

Select material adapted from *Growing in God's Love: A Story Bible* and *Growing in God's Love: A Story Bible Curriculum*. Used by permission of Westminster John Knox Press.

Book design by Ann DeVilbiss
Cover design by Mary Ann Smith

Library of Congress Cataloging-in-Publication Data is on file at the Library of Congress, Washington, DC.

ISBN: 978-0-664-26918-0 (paperback)
ISBN: 978-1-646-98441-1 (ebook)

Most Westminster John Knox Press books are available at special quantity discounts when purchased in bulk by corporations, organizations, and special-interest groups. For more information, please e-mail Special Sales@wjkbooks.com.

Contents

Making the Most of This Book	vii
The Devotions	
Part of God's Story (*Psalm 19*)	2
The Most Important Thing (*Deuteronomy 6:4–9*)	4
It Was Good (*Genesis 1:1–2:4a*)	6
From the Earth (*Genesis 2:4b–22*)	8
Seed Stories (*Luke 8:4–15*)	10
God Is There (*Genesis 6:11–22; 7:17–8:12; 9:8–17*)	12
Different Is Good (*Genesis 11:1–9*)	14
Feeling at Home (*Genesis 12:1–4a; 17:1–16*)	16
Why Laugh? (*Genesis 18:1–15; 21:1–7*)	18
No Perfect Families (*Genesis 16:1–16; 21:8–21*)	20
Sibling Rivalry (*Genesis 27:1–38*)	22
Less Is More (*Matthew 13:31–33*)	24
Wrestling with God (*Genesis 32:22–32*)	26
What to Do with Envy (*Genesis 29:1–30; 30:22–24*)	28
Dreams from God (*Genesis 37:1–36; 41:1–40*)	30
Working for Good (*Genesis 42:1–23; 45:1–15*)	32
Women Who Resisted (*Exodus 1:8–2:10*)	34

Holy Places (*Exodus 3:1–12*)	36
Let My People Go (*Exodus 11; 12:21–36*)	38
Trusting in Enough (*Exodus 16:1–31*)	40
Rules That Help Everyone (*Exodus 20:1–21*)	42
No Fair! (*Matthew 20:1–16*)	44
Being Brave (*Joshua 2:1–24*)	46
Choosing God (*Joshua 24:1–24*)	48
Friends Who Help (*Job 4:1–9; 6:1–4, 14–17*)	50
Chosen Family (*Ruth 1:1–19a*)	52
No King, Just God (*1 Samuel 8:1–22*)	54
God Looks at the Heart (*1 Samuel 16:1–13*)	56
A Good Neighbor (*Luke 10:25–37*)	58
Where God Lives (*2 Samuel 7:1–9*)	60
Telling Hard Truths (*Amos 5:10–24*)	62
The Pouting Prophet (*Jonah 3:1–5; 4:1–11*)	64
God Is with Us (*Isaiah 7:10–16; 9:2–7; 43:1–7*)	66
What Mary Knew (*Luke 1:26–56*)	68
An Ordinary, Extraordinary Baby (*Luke 2:1–7*)	70
Visitors from Near and Far (*Luke 2:8–20; Matthew 2:1–12*)	72
Learning from One Another (*Luke 2:39–52*)	74
Jesus Is Baptized (*Luke 3:1–17*)	76
It's Very Tempting (*Luke 4:1–12*)	78
Drop Everything (*Matthew 4:18–22; 10:1–4*)	80
Living Water (*John 4:1–30*)	82
Jesus Heals (*John 4:46–54*)	84
Everybody Counts (*Luke 15:1–32*)	86
Faithful Steps (*Matthew 6:25–34*)	88
Seeing Jesus (*Matthew 25:31–40*)	90
A Different Sort of King (*Luke 19:29–40*)	92
Eat, Drink, and Remember (*Luke 22:7–20*)	94
Jesus Dies (*Luke 23:13–49*)	96
Jesus Lives (*Luke 24:1–12*)	98
Faith and Doubt (*John 20:19–31*)	100
Speaking in the Spirit (*Acts 2:1–41*)	102
Enough for Everyone (*Acts 2:42–47; 4:32–35*)	104
From Persecutor to Preacher (*Acts 8:1–3; 9:1–19*)	106
Part of the Body (*1 Corinthians 12:12–31*)	108
All Cheering for You (*Hebrews 11:23–12:2*)	110

Making the Most of This Book

For busy parents, the list of things we want to do with and for our families is generally infinitely longer than the amount of time and energy we have to accomplish such things. Investing in the faith development of our kids—and ourselves—often falls by the wayside in the midst of so many other priorities. Getting everybody out the door for an hour of church on Sundays is overwhelming enough—and might even be something you've chosen to set aside in favor of more peaceful family time.

This devotional book is designed to make meaningful conversations about faith a simple addition to your family's schedule. The devotions are short and have flexible components so that you can determine what works for your family. Use these devotions over dinner or before bedtime, daily or once a week, to guide your family in exploring how God has been at work in our world since the time of creation and how we can be a part of God's work today. You don't need to be an expert on the Bible or a perfect example of Christian faith. This book is an opportunity for adults and kids alike to discover more about God, one another, and faithful living in God's world. Each devotion involves three components:

SCRIPTURE

Bible stories are the starting point for each devotion—not because the Bible answers all our questions but because it invites us to wrestle with ideas, choices, and challenges just as God's people living thousands of years ago did. These are the stories that our faith was built on, and while times are very different, God's relationship with humanity is a story that goes on and on. Engaging our imagination while reading Scripture allows us to consider what these stories have meant to people across time and space and discover their meaning for our lives today. Some stories may be familiar to you, learned in Sunday school or from a preacher's sermon, while others may seem brand new.

Begin by reading the focus Scripture aloud, either from *Growing in God's Love: A Story Bible* (page numbers are provided) or from the Bible translation of your choice. You may want to refer to both versions of the story, letting younger children look at the illustrations in the story Bible while an adult or older child reads the Scripture passage. Practice together how to locate Scriptures by book, chapter, and verse.

Growing in God's Love: A Story Bible and *The Westminster Study Bible: New Revised Standard Version Updated Edition*, referenced in the development of these devotions, both reflect the recent thinking and writing of contemporary biblical scholars, so you may see some new interpretations of familiar stories. The devotions are ordered to give readers a sense of the Bible's overall narrative, how one story leads to another in a journey of faith that is both part of history and outside of it. Some devotions featuring Jesus' parables are interspersed among devotions featuring

Old Testament stories, both for variety and to emphasize connections between Jesus' storytelling and his Jewish tradition.

You'll notice that more devotions are drawn from the Bible's first two books, Genesis and Exodus, than other books in the Old Testament. This is because these stories are foundational for Jewish people's sense of identity and thus the religious formation of Jesus and the Scripture that our two traditions share. Plus, it's hard to find any section of the Bible that features more on family dynamics than Genesis 12–50! Themes that emerge in the epic story of Abraham and Sarah and the generations that follow make excellent conversation starters for modern families.

REFLECTION

Following the Scripture, read the reflection out loud. One person can read, or you can pass the book around and take turns reading. Each reflection aims to provide context for understanding the Scripture's meaning and connect the age-old story to our lives today. Such connections may be very practical, concerning how we relate to other people, or more spiritual, concerning our identity as God's children and how God works in the world.

Each devotion is around three hundred words and should take no more than a minute or two to read. They are written to engage with adults and kids alike, though you might need to explain some words to younger elementary children. Some devotions highlight a key word that is important for conversations about faith.

RESPONSE

You will also find in each devotion three opportunities to respond to what you've read together: Discuss, Discover, and Do.

- "Discuss" is a question or prompt that each person can answer. Invite each person to share their thoughts—there are no wrong answers! Let conversation flow from there for as long as your schedule allows.
- "Discover" is a challenge to investigate something further—maybe in a book or on a map, maybe somewhere else in your Bible, maybe by phoning a friend or searching the internet.
- "Do" is a suggested action you can take to make the devotion's lesson tangible. It might be something creative and crafty you can do at home, or it could be a way of serving people out in the world. You might be able to do it right away, or you may need to make a plan to do it another time.

You may want to try all three—Discuss, Discover, and Do—or you can read the options and pick one together. Figure out what works for you based on the ages, attention spans, and interests of your family members!

Close your special time together by reading the prayer provided or letting someone offer their own prayer. Enjoy this time of listening together for the ways that God continues to speak, through the Bible and through our lives.

The Devotions

Part of God's Story

Read Psalm 19
or "Listening for God" (*Story Bible*, p. 163)

Did you know that we have something in common with people who lived thousands of years ago? Farmers who hoped for rain, parents celebrating a new baby, children wondering where the sun goes at night . . . we are all part of God's story! Everyone who talks to God, wonders about God, asks what God wants—everyone who God created—is part of God's story.

People have been talking about God since before there were things to write with. Some parts of God's story have been written down for us to read, and other parts we discover as we go, following God just as people have been doing since the beginning.

The Bible is a collection of writings about God and God's people. Some people say it's like a library, with books of history, books of poetry, books of wise teachings, and more. Some people say the Bible is like a quilt made up of many colors and kinds of fabrics, with threads that run throughout and tie the stories together. The Bible is the work of many different people, all sharing their ideas about God and stories of how God and people relate to each other.

The part of the Bible that Christians call the Old Testament is also Jewish Scripture, full of wisdom about how God's people were to live together and how they were to treat other people. These were the stories and lessons Jesus learned growing up as a Jewish child. The New Testament includes stories of Jesus' life and teachings, plus letters and other things written by Jesus' first followers.

The Bible contains a lot of stories about God, but it alone cannot contain God's story—there's too much to say, too much to learn. As your family reads and prays together, remember that you are part of something big—a God-sized story that goes on and on.

Discuss: What do you wonder about God?

Discover: How many Bibles are in your house? How are they different from one another?

Do: Use pictures and words from an old magazine to make a collage about God. We don't have a picture of God, but all our ideas and images together show us parts of God's story.

God, thank you for making us part of your story. Help us look for you and think of you everywhere we go. Amen.

The Most Important Thing

Read Deuteronomy 6:4-9
or "The Most Important Thing to Remember"
(*Story Bible*, p. 168)

Do you have a list of house rules? If so, some might be very general, like "be kind" or "tell the truth." Others might be very specific to your house, like "Keep the back door locked so that Fluffy can't escape."

The first five books of the Old Testament are called the Torah, because in addition to stories, this section includes many "teaching" instructions for how God's people should live. Some are very specific for certain people in a certain time and place—things like how to prevent skin diseases and the right way to slaughter livestock. Today, we have specific rules for things like driving cars responsibly and being safe online.

There are also laws about treating one another fairly and taking care of people in need—things that are always important for everyone. The most important commandment is something some Jewish people still say twice a day, when they wake up and when they go to bed. It's called the Shema, which means "hear," because that is the first word of this passage of Scripture in Hebrew:

> "Hear, O Israel: the Lord is our God, the Lord alone. You shall love the Lord your God with all your heart and with all your soul and with all your might." (vv. 4–5)

The verses following these say to hold these words close, reading and discussing them often and teaching them to the next generation. Verse 8 says to put these words on your hand, on your forehead, and by the door of your house. Jews throughout the centuries have written the Shema on tiny scrolls and placed them in little boxes to use while praying and to hang by the door. The Shema is also the commandment Jesus quotes when he is asked what the most important commandment is.

This commandment to know God and love God with everything we have must be pretty important! That's why God's people today, young and old, of every generation, keep reading and studying the Bible, gathering together to worship, and talking together about how to love God and other people the best we can. We can't do it alone! We need to help one another remember what is most important.

Discuss: How can we love God with every part of ourselves?

Discover: Read Matthew 22:37–40. What did Jesus say was the second most important commandment? Can you find where in the Old Testament that commandment comes from?

Do: Have each family member write the Shema on a sheet of paper and decorate it. Younger kids can just write "Love God" or color a heart. Hang these signs around your house where you will see them every day.

Dear God, help us know and trust that you alone are God. Help us love you in everything we do and keep learning from one another how to love more. Amen.

It Was Good

Read Genesis 1:1-2:4a
Or "How God Made Everything" (*Story Bible*, pp. 20-21)

Every culture has at least one story about how the world began. In the Bible, there are two, written by two very different storytellers. In Genesis 1, the storyteller imagines the whole, huge universe and how God spoke everything into being.

This creation story tells how the world was created in seven days, with God bringing order to a world that was previously a formless, chaotic, watery void. God completes certain tasks each day, making distinctions and separations between light and dark, earth and sky, water and land, sea animals and flying animals. On the sixth day, God creates land animals and humans but makes a very special distinction for humans: humans are made in God's image and given the responsibility of caring for the animals.

Notice the repetitions and refrains, the rhythms the storyteller used to describe God's process of creating the world and resting on the seventh day. Each act of creation begins with God saying, "Let there be . . ." or "Let the . . ." and later, God seeing that the creation was good. This storyteller might have been a priest who related to God through the patterns and prayers of daily worship and weekly rest. We can see their attention to detail and awe at creation. Clearly, they love God and the world God made. One of the words that is repeated is the Hebrew word *tov*, which means "good or beautiful."

This story doesn't give a scientific explanation for how things happened. (As Genesis 1:6 suggests, many ancient people thought the earth was flat and covered by a dome that sometimes let water through in the form of rain!) Rather, the purpose of the story is to show how God is connected with creation—from the smallest insect to the largest animal, from the tiniest mushroom to the largest redwood tree—and how humans were made good, in God's image, and charged with caring for the beautiful world God created.

> **Discuss:** What do you think it means to be created "in the image of God"?
>
> **Discover:** Research some new ways your family can help take better care of the planet.
>
> **Do:** Go on a walk, pointing out to one another the things you see that God created and saying *"ki-tov"*—it's good.

Dear God, what a beautiful world you made. Help us see your image and goodness in all people and care for your good creation. Amen.

From the Earth

Read Genesis 2:4b-22
Or "We Were All Farmers Once" (*Story Bible*, pp. 22-23)

The second creation story in the Bible is very different from the first. Rather than starting in a chaotic void of space, Genesis 2 starts with dry, barren land. There were no plants, no bodies of water. Into this landscape, a stream bubbles up from under the ground, and from the moistened earth, God forms a human—literally, an earthling—into which God breathes the breath of life. Only after the human is made does God create plants—a garden and trees, many sources of food the human can grow and pick and eat.

It is also in this story that God first notices something *not good* about creation: "It is not good that the man should be alone; I will make him a helper as his partner" (v. 18). This is when animals are created in this story—as part of God's quest to find a good helper for the human. But God realizes that to be an equal partner, the helper must also be human.

This storyteller isn't focused on the daily order of creation or the role of humans as being in charge of creation. This storyteller is more concerned with the connection of humans to the land and to one another. Instead of a priest, this ancient writer was probably a farmer who wanted people to remember that this rich, dark soil from which humans were created was the same rich, dark soil in which they grew their food.

Today, most of us are far removed from the food we eat. Rather than growing fruits, vegetables, and grains ourselves or buying them directly from farmers, we often live very far away from the people who work hard tilling, seeding, and picking our food—not to mention packing, shipping, and processing the food. We probably don't know much about them or their lives. This story reminds us that we are all connected and that God doesn't want anyone to be alone but to partner with families, friends, coworkers, and neighbors to care for our world together.

Discuss: How does it feel to imagine God kneading and forming you like clay or dough?

Discover: Read labels to see where your food comes from, and try to learn about the people who grow and package the foods you eat.

Do: Find a place you can volunteer as a family to help share food with those in need—through organizations like Second Harvest or the Society of Saint Andrew or via a local community garden or food pantry.

Dear God, help us remember that we are all connected to one another and to the earth. Amen.

Seed Stories

Read Luke 8:4-15
Or "The Sower" (*Story Bible*, pp. 210-11)

Because Jesus was Jewish, he would have known these creation stories and other stories from the part of the Bible we call the Old Testament. Most of the people he taught knew those stories too. They also knew a lot more about growing food than most of us do today, so when Jesus told stories, he often used people and examples from nature in these stories, which we call parables.

Parables invite us to think and to imagine life differently. They ask us to look at our own lives, to think about how we are living, and to think about how God wants us to live. Parables help us consider the choices we can make.

In Jesus' parable about the sower, we see a farmer throwing seed all over the place—on the path, into the bushes, and onto rocky soil that wasn't cleared or prepared for planting. The people listening to Jesus might have laughed, because clearly this wasn't a very good farmer! Rather than being careful to put seeds in the good soil where they were most likely to grow, he was throwing seed around willy-nilly, wasting good seed!

Jesus explains that the seed is like God's loving message to them. People hear it but aren't all ready to receive it in a way that will grow and bloom inside them. Sometimes our hearts feel hard like rocks, and we don't want to hear about love right then. Sometimes we hear but soon forget. The good news is that God throws love around like crazy. There's always another chance.

Sometimes Jesus' parables were confusing, and even his closest followers complained that they didn't understand. Parables can be kind of messy—just like the sower throwing his seed around wildly and just like God, throwing love over all of us, all the time.

Discuss: How does your heart feel right now?

Discover: Read two other Scripture passages that talk about sowing seed: Isaiah 55:10–13 and 2 Corinthians 9:6–11.

Do: Go outside and scatter breadcrumbs or birdseed as wildly as you can. Will birds or animals be able to eat the food where it landed?

God, let us throw love around as wildly as you do. Amen.

God Is There

Read Genesis 6:11-22; 7:17-8:12; 9:8-17
Or "When the World Started Over Again"
(*Story Bible*, pp. 24-25)

Like creation stories, every culture also has a story about a time when people were afraid the world was going to end. People didn't know why natural disasters like floods, earthquakes, or tornadoes happened, and—just like today—they didn't know why some people lost everything in the disaster and others didn't. Stories can help people make sense of things when life feels sad and confusing. The story of Noah and his family in Genesis chapters 6 through 9 is, at its core, a story about loss and beginning again.

Imagine looking out your window and seeing the rain fall for hours on end—days, even. You might wonder if it would ever stop. If your family had to go somewhere higher to stay dry and safe, what would you most want to take with you? Your pets? Favorite toys or books? Things that remind you of special memories and people you love? You might be scared and wonder when you will feel safe again.

Sometimes, life feels scary and out of control, and it has nothing to do with the weather. Changes like moving houses or schools can shake our foundations. Loved ones getting sick or dying can break your heart and make you feel as if nothing will ever feel right again. It takes a long time to feel secure and happy again after you lose something or someone important. But eventually, you do.

The story of Noah and the flood ends with God making a covenant—a promise—to Noah and to the whole world to always be with us, no matter what hap-

> A **covenant** is a very serious, very important agreement or promise.

pens. Disasters will come, but we will never be cut off from God. God is there to comfort us and give us hope. If we need a reminder of that, God says to look at the rainbow and know that even when it feels as if the world is ending, as if the rain and pain will never stop, the sun *will* come out again.

Discuss: When have you experienced fear, sadness, or loss? Did you feel God there with you?

Discover: Visit the website of a disaster relief organization, such as Presbyterian Disaster Assistance, to find out where people in the world are currently experiencing a disaster. Pray for those people and think about ways you could help them.

Do: Paint with watercolors and talk about what the rainbow means to you.

Dear God, when the waters of life flood over us and we can barely keep our heads up, help us remember your promise to always be with us. Amen.

Different Is Good

Read Genesis 11:1-9
Or "God's Big Plan" (*Story Bible*, pp. 164-65)

Do you find it easier to work together with people who are all like you, or do you like collaborating with people who are different from you?

Early in the Bible, there is a story about a community of people who were all alike, all speaking one language and making big plans for themselves, and how God decided to intervene. The people liked being alike, so they decided to build a big city with a huge skyscraper so that they could stay together and never leave—but God had an even bigger plan. God wanted people to learn to live with others who are different from them.

Think back to the first time you can remember meeting someone who was different from you. What did you notice? Was it the color of their skin, the language they spoke, or the place they were born? Were their abilities different from yours? Was their faith tradition or their church not the same as yours?

It can sometimes be hard to understand, communicate, and work together when people have different ways of doing things and bring new and different ideas to the table. Sometimes we'd rather just do things *our* way. So we put up walls—emotionally and sometimes even physically—to keep other people out. Differences can bring change and might even make us change our minds. That can feel scary. But listening to one another, learning from one another, and figuring out a plan together can make us all better. Diversity is part of the wonderful world God created, and God knew that we're better off together than we are apart.

Discuss: How are people in your school, workplace, or neighborhood different from one another? What do you appreciate about people who are different from you?

Discover: Learn a few phrases in another language or consider studying a language as a family using an app or live classes.

Do: Create a welcome basket for a family that is new to your neighborhood. Introduce yourselves with a letter or drawings, and remember to include something for all members of the family, even pets.

God, it's amazing how many different kinds of people you made! Help us work together to be the diverse community you want us to be. Amen.

Feeling at Home

Read Genesis 12:1-4a; 17:1-16
Or "Abram and Sarai Find a New Home" (*Story Bible*, p. 26)

Do you live in the same town as your grandparents or cousins? In ancient times—and for most of history—it was not common to leave your family behind and head out to a new place, but Abram and Sarai did. They made this huge move because God asked them to. God made a covenant with them to be their God and to be with them always; in return, Abram and Sarai promised to always remember that God is their God. God told them that they would produce a new nation: a people more numerous than the stars in the sky, and God changed their names to Abraham and Sarah to reflect the new identity God had given them.

People still make huge moves like Abraham and Sarah, migrating from one land to another. All over the earth, people travel great distances in search of safety and the resources they need to make a good life. They may have to leave home because of war or violence, a famine, or other disaster. With no guarantee of what they will find elsewhere, they

> **Migration** means moving in search of food or work. Immigration means moving into a new country.

have hope that a new place will be better than what they've known. Your own ancestors may have been immigrants, moving to a new country in hope of a better life. Or they might have been moved from their homeland against their will, forced to seek freedom in a country they never chose. We don't know everyone's story, but we can have empathy for those making difficult journeys.

Imagine what it must be like to move somewhere you've never been, where you might not even know the language. Think about what makes a place feel like home and what would help you to feel at home in a new place. Maybe God can use you to make someone's journey a little easier.

Discuss: When have you gone somewhere you'd never been before? How did it feel to be in a new place?

Discover: Get out a map or globe and trace the paths immigrants in your town might have taken to get there. Then consider the paths your own ancestors might have taken to get to a new homeland.

Do: Contact a refugee organization in your area and ask what you can do to help immigrants in your town.

Dear God, open our eyes to see people's hard journeys, and help us welcome them to a new home. Amen.

Why Laugh?

Read Genesis 18:1-15; 21:1-7
Or "God Made Sarah Laugh" (*Story Bible*, p. 50)

God had promised Abraham and Sarah that they would be the father and mother of so many descendants that they wouldn't be able to count them all. But the couple waited a long time, and God hadn't even given them one child, much less a multitude! As the years passed and Sarah became an old woman, the possibility of children seemed less and less likely. This is why the mysterious visitor's announcement that Sarah would have a baby in the next year seemed so absurd that Sarah laughed out loud.

The visitor must have seemed very strange when he asked, with a straight face, "Why are you laughing?" It was a joke, right? Didn't he know that old people didn't have babies? But he was serious and asked Sarah an important question: "Is anything too wonderful for the Lord?" (18:14). Is there anything God can't do?

This question is at the heart of what it means to have faith. We trust that God is powerful and wants good things for us. Sometimes, bad things happen, and we don't know why, but we do know God is with us through it all, even when it feels silly to hope for better things.

Sarah thought it was pretty silly to think an old woman could have a baby. But it happened! Less than a year after the mysterious visitors came, Sarah got pregnant and gave birth to a little boy she named Isaac, which means "laughter." God kept the promise to make Abraham and Sarah the ancestors of a great nation. God's way of keeping the covenant is often unexpected, but with God nothing is impossible.

Discuss: Have you ever seen something happen that you had thought was impossible?

Discover: There are other stories in the Bible of women having babies when no one thought they could. Can you remember or find any of their stories? (Hint: look in 1 Samuel 1 and Luke 1.)

Do: Try to make each other laugh with jokes or silly faces. Whoever causes the biggest laugh wins!

Tell us, God: Is there anything you can't do? Help us have hope, even when things feel impossible. Amen.

No Perfect Families

Read Genesis 16:1-16; 21:8-21
Or "A Family with a Big Disagreement" and "A Family Changes Its Shape" (*Story Bible*, pp. 44-47)

A new baby always changes things, but Abraham and Sarah's family had experienced some other challenges even before Isaac was born. Abraham had a son with Sarah's servant, Hagar, which made Sarah feel jealous and angry that Hagar was pregnant when she was not. After Isaac was born, Sarah worried that Hagar's son, Ishmael, would become more important than Isaac. This was not the perfect family Sarah had dreamed of when God promised her many descendants.

Turns out, there's no such thing as a perfect family. Families come in all shapes and sizes and may change in ways that we don't want. Sometimes families live all together in one house, and sometimes family members live separately. Sometimes we don't get along, and sometimes we feel close. Sometimes things are going well for some members of the family, while others are struggling. And all these things can change—sometimes before you even know what's happening.

In every situation, relationships between family members can be complicated. It may be tempting to take sides, but no one is perfect—not even this family that God made a special covenant with. Sarah was unkind to Hagar, who had no power in the situation, and Abraham took no responsibility for his actions, instead sending Hagar and Ishmael away to fend for themselves.

Nevertheless, in the midst of all this imperfection, God was with each person. God was with Sarah in her anger and sadness. God was with Hagar, who was terrified in the wilderness. God kept the covenant with Abraham and even promised Hagar that she would have a multitude of descendants too.

When God spoke to Hagar in the wilderness, she gave God the name *El-roi*, which means "God who sees." God still sees us and cares for us and our families, no matter what we're going through or how things change.

Discuss: How has your family changed over time? What has been the hardest change?

Discover: What disagreements or changes are happening in your community right now? How can you learn more about the issues involved and take action to care for people who are hurt by the situation?

Do: Create a big family photo collage. Talk together about who is in your family, near and far away, and who feels like family, even if they aren't related to you.

El-roi, thank you for seeing us with loving eyes and being with us always, no matter what may change. Amen.

Sibling Rivalry

Read Genesis 27:1-38
Or "Esau and Jacob Both Want Their Share"
(*Story Bible*, pp. 32-33)

How many kids are in your family? If there is more than one, chances are there is some sibling rivalry. It's normal for siblings to fight sometimes, to feel jealousy or anger. Sometimes, being far apart in age can spark conflict, since your interests and activities are likely different. (For example, a younger sibling might take an older sibling's favorite sweatshirt and "decorate" it with permanent marker.) Being close in age has its problems too, since there may be more competition between you. (One sibling might "borrow" that favorite sweatshirt and get more compliments on it!)

When Isaac grew up, he and his wife, Rebekah, had twin sons who fought with each other even before they were born. (You can read about that in Genesis 25.) Jacob and Esau had very different interests and were also very competitive with each other. Much of the rivalry between Jacob and Esau happened because of rules at that time, which gave preference to the oldest son. If you know any twins, they likely tease each other about who was born first—generally by a matter of minutes—but for Jacob and Esau, their birth order made a huge difference in the inheritance they would receive from their father.

Rebekah and Jacob saw those rules as unfair and tried to even the playing field by tricking Isaac when he was old and couldn't see well. That doesn't exactly seem fair either, and their actions hurt Esau.

Have you ever heard the phrase "there are two sides to every story?" Some conflicts are more complicated than a stolen (or borrowed) sweatshirt, and they are harder to work through. When family members, countries, or religious groups have fought for a long time, it becomes harder to say who started it or who is more at fault. Reconciliation takes humility, patience, and compassion—things we can develop by praying to God and practicing every chance we get.

> **Reconciliation** means resolving differences and making peace.

Discuss: Who do you think was right or wrong in Jacob and Esau's story? How might they have solved their conflict instead?

Discover: What strategies can you find for working through conflict with family members or friends? One example is to take turns listening really carefully to understand why the other person feels the way they do.

Do: Are there any rules in your home, school, or country that you think are unfair? Write a letter to those who make the rules, explaining your position and noting what you would like to see changed.

Lord, help us work through our differences with patience and kindness. Amen.

Less Is More

Read Matthew 13:31-33
Or "Something Big from Something Small"
(*Story Bible*, pp. 224-25)

Would you say humans are big or small? Compared to ants and germs, we're pretty big. Compared to a mountain, the sun, or the whole universe, though, we're pretty small.

We know God is big. God created the universe, after all, and everything in it. Compared to God, we definitely seem small, and yet we matter to God and can do things that matter in our world. Jesus said as much in the parables he told. Many of Jesus' parables talked about the kingdom of God or the realm of heaven, which isn't actually a place but a vision of what the world could be if everyone lived as God wants.

The realm of heaven sounds pretty big, but Jesus said that it is like a mustard seed. Mustard seeds are very small, but the bushes that grow from them can get pretty big, and Jesus even imagines this tiny thing growing into a tree big enough for birds to nest in! In God's vision for the world, small things yield enormous results.

Jesus also said that the realm of heaven is like yeast. Just a small amount can leaven many pounds of flour and turn it into a fluffy dough that can be baked into bread to feed many people.

God has always been especially fond of things and people that often get overlooked or are considered less important. We see this in stories in Genesis, when God takes special care of younger siblings like Jacob, and all through Scripture, when God reminds people again and again to care about the poor, the immigrant, the sick—whoever is easily overlooked or cast aside.

You may feel little sometimes. Maybe you're the youngest in your family or get less attention than other people. Maybe you wonder if you'll ever do anything that really matters. Just remember that God is always using people like you to do big things. Like a little mustard seed or a little bit of yeast, even small things are a big deal in God's world.

> **Discuss:** What other examples can you think of where someone or something little and seemingly unimportant makes a big impact?
>
> **Discover:** Find the "Cosmic Eye" video on YouTube to see the scale of biggest and smallest things known to human science.
>
> **Do:** Bake bread together. Remember that people in Jesus' time didn't have instant yeast, as we do today. Their yeast would have been more like the starter people still use to bake sourdough bread. Whatever kind of bread you bake, think about the impact each small ingredient has on the recipe.

God, you are so big, and yet you choose the smallest, the youngest, the cast aside to be most important in your kingdom. Amen.

Wrestling with God

Read Genesis 32:22-32
Or "When Things Get Really Scary" (*Story Bible*, pp. 34-35)

Have you ever wrestled with another person? What about with an idea? You think about something, but you're not really sure. Your mind goes back and forth, considering the pros and cons of the idea. Does it make sense? Is it right?

Jacob and Esau probably wrestled a lot growing up as brothers who didn't really get along. But after running away in fear after he'd made Esau very mad, Jacob had a lot more wrestling to do. Many years had passed, and the brothers were preparing to see each other again for the first time since Jacob had tricked and betrayed Esau. The night before they were to meet, Jacob sat down beside a river and wrestled with his plan. Was it dangerous to meet Esau again? Maybe Esau would still be so angry that he would kill him on the spot. Jacob wanted to restore their relationship, and Esau had agreed to see him, but there was still a chance it could make everything worse.

In the middle of all this mind wrestling, a mysterious being appeared and wrestled Jacob physically, until Jacob was injured and desperate and the sun was starting to rise. Jacob asked the being to bless him—maybe he thought the being could provide magical protection for his scary meeting with Esau. Instead, the being blessed Jacob with a new name—Israel, which means "wrestles with God."

We can still wrestle with God today. Maybe not physically, but we wrestle with God every time we ask ourselves what God wants us to do, or what God is like, or what words about God in the Bible mean. Some people might say it's wrong to wrestle with God, to question ideas about God, but Jacob might remind us that wrestling with God brings blessings—blessings like understanding, closeness, and courage to face whatever scares us.

> Jacob's new name, **Israel**, also became a name for the Hebrew people descended from him—*Israelites* or the "people of Israel." Much later, they became known as Jews.

Discuss: Have you ever wrestled with God? What was it like?

Discover: What big gift did Jacob bring for Esau to show him how sorry he was? Read Genesis 32:13–15 and think about why this was such a valuable gift in Jacob and Esau's time and place.

Do: Think about what meaningful name or words of blessing you would like God to give you. Write it on a piece of paper or paint it on a rock to keep and remind you of who you strive to be.

God, thank you for welcoming our questions and struggles. It is a blessing to wrestle with you. Amen.

What to Do with Envy

Read Genesis 29:1-30; 30:22-24
Or "Two Sisters: Leah and Rachel" (*Story Bible*, pp. 54-55)

Things were pretty different in the time of Jacob's story (around two thousand years before Jesus was born). It was common for people's parents to decide who their children would marry—often someone they were related to, like a cousin, so that the family tribe could grow bigger and stronger. It was common for men to have more than one wife so that the family could have many children. Jacob became the father of thirteen children—one daughter and twelve sons—but the process of building such a big family wasn't easy.

Jacob fell in love with Rachel but had to marry her older sister, Leah, first. You can imagine how that made Leah feel! Leah gave birth to four sons, though, and Leah's and Rachel's servants had many children too. Rachel wanted children, but she couldn't get pregnant. Each sister had something the other wanted: Leah had children but was sad, knowing that Jacob had wanted to marry Rachel first. Rachel had Jacob's love, but no children. They were jealous of each other.

Jealousy, also called envy, is common among siblings, and it was common in the families we read about in Genesis: between Jacob and Esau, Leah and Rachel, and among Jacob's thirteen children too (as we'll see in the next story). Envy can make people do terrible things.

Envy can also give us information about what we truly desire. When we want something someone else has, we can ask ourselves why we want that thing. Does that thing have special value for us, or do we really want the attention or status it could bring us? Maybe what we really want is connection with others, or maybe we find we already have what we really need. Envy is an uncomfortable feeling, but it doesn't have to poison our relationships. It's our choice what to do with that difficult feeling.

Discuss: When have you felt envious? What could that experience tell you about what you truly want?

Discover: Envy is traditionally associated with the color green. Try to find out why that is.

Do: Think about things you have that other people might want or need more than you do. Consider giving something away to someone who needs it more.

Lord, forgive us when our desire for things we don't have makes us treat others badly. Show us how to be truly happy. Amen.

Dreams from God

Read Genesis 37:1-36; 41:1-40
Or "Joseph and His Brothers" and "Joseph Helps Out in Egypt"
(*Story Bible*, pp. 38-41)

Do you remember your dreams when you wake up in the morning? Do you tell your family over breakfast about the silly or scary things that happened in your dreams?

Joseph was a kid who dreamed vivid dreams and had a gift for understanding what they meant—but maybe he should have thought twice about telling his family about them.

Joseph was his dad's favorite child because he had been born to Rachel, who had been barren for so long. Joseph's older brothers were already jealous of him because Jacob gave him lots of special attention and a special present: a fancy robe. So when Joseph told his brothers about his dreams in which they all bowed down to him, they'd had enough. All that special treatment had gone to Joseph's head, they thought!

The brothers sold Joseph to some slave traders who took him to Egypt. Joseph became a servant in a powerful man's home and then ended up in prison. Things seemed to be getting worse and worse for Joseph—until his fellow prisoners discovered his gift for interpreting dreams and told Pharaoh, who'd been having some troubling dreams of his own.

Joseph realized something that he might not have known when he was still a kid at home with his brothers: his gift was from God, and God was with him the whole time that he was suffering as a slave and in prison. Joseph used his gift wisely to interpret Pharaoh's dreams and help Egypt plan for a coming disaster by storing up food for a time when there wouldn't be enough. Pharaoh was so impressed with Joseph's wisdom that he made Joseph his right-hand man, the second most powerful person in all Egypt.

Ask God for wisdom to discover and use your gifts well. You may not be able to interpret dreams, but you have other gifts that God can use to make the world better.

Discuss: Why do you think God gave Joseph the gift of interpreting dreams? What gifts has God given you?

Discover: Psychologists have some theories about why we dream and what certain dreams might mean. Find an article or video about the science of dreaming.

Do: Write your name in the middle of a sheet of paper. Around your name, draw pictures of the things you enjoy and the things you are good at.

God, thank you for the gifts you've given each of us. Help us use them wisely and know that you are always with us. Amen.

Working for Good

Read Genesis 42:1-23; 45:1-15
Or "Joseph Helps His Brothers" (*Story Bible*, pp. 42-43)

Do you ever wonder why bad things happen? People have been wondering that forever. When someone dies, the people who miss them ask why? When natural disasters like fires, floods, and earthquakes happen, people ask why? Joseph may have asked why? when he was sold into slavery and stuck in prison, and his brothers probably asked why? when the famine that Joseph had predicted would come to Egypt also came to Canaan.

The brothers thought they had an answer to why? when Joseph at first refused to help them (though they didn't know it was Joseph). "We're being punished for what we did to our brother!" they cried. People back then and even today sometimes think bad things happen as punishment for things we've done wrong.

When Joseph finally reveals who he is to his brothers, he tells them not to worry; they did a bad thing selling him into slavery, but God used him to save lives. He said, "Even though you intended to do harm to me, God intended it for good" (50:20). God would never want someone to hurt someone else, but when Joseph's brothers chose to sell him away, God found a way to use that bad choice to do something good.

God is always at work, wanting good things for us and calling us to be good to one another. This doesn't mean that the bad things don't hurt, but it can give us hope in difficult and scary times.

Joseph knew God was present with him. This confidence helped him to view his life—even the bad parts—through the lens of faith and see how God could use him to save lives, to feed hungry people in a time of crisis, and even to bring his family back together.

Discuss: What is something good that came out of a bad situation your family has experienced?

Discover: People asked Jesus if bad things happened because people sinned. Read his answer in John 9:1–5. (He talks about this idea in Matthew 5:45b and Luke 13:1–5 too.)

Do: Help out someone who is going through a hard time right now. God can use you to bring goodness into their bad situation.

God, thank you for making good things come out of bad situations. You are always working, even when we don't understand. Amen.

Women Who Resisted

Read Exodus 1:8-2:10
Or "Miriam Hides Moses" (*Story Bible*, p. 56)

You've probably heard the story of Moses—the baby who floated down a river in a basket, grew up in the palace like a prince of Egypt, and then led the Hebrew people out of slavery and into the promised land. Moses is one of the great heroes of the Bible, but his story never would have happened without some brave women who stood up to Pharaoh first.

The Hebrews were the descendants of Joseph and his brothers who had moved to Egypt during the famine, but after so many years, Egyptians saw them as just a group of foreigners who were a threat to "real" Egyptians. To keep their population from growing more, Pharaoh ordered that the midwives—women skilled in helping other women give birth—should stealthily kill the newborn Hebrew boys as soon as they were born. Instead, the midwives defied Pharaoh by letting the babies live and saying that the Hebrew women gave birth before they could get there.

Pharaoh then said that anyone who finds a baby Hebrew boy should throw it in the river. Moses's mother defied Pharaoh by hiding her baby instead. Pharaoh's daughter defied her father by rescuing the baby and keeping it as her own. Moses's sister defied Pharaoh by taking the baby back to her mother, who the princess hired as a nursemaid to take care of Moses!

Obeying Pharaoh would have been the safe, lawful thing to do. But instead, each of these women risked getting in big trouble in order to save lives. They resisted. They said no. They pushed back.

When leaders and laws hurt people, it is tempting to stay quiet, especially if you aren't being hurt yourself. It seems easier to just go along with powerful people when they are doing things you know are wrong. It feels safer to be on the bully's side than the victim's. But when people are using their power to hurt others, the right thing to do is resist. Say no. Push back.

> **Resisting** means to push back, to not go along with.

Discuss: Have you ever spoken out against something you knew was wrong?

Discover: Learn about what Martin Luther King Jr. called "nonviolent resistance."

Do: Explore resistance in the scientific sense by pressing the palms of your hands against someone else's and pushing. Take turns holding firm and giving way.

God, thank you for brave women and men who have resisted evil. Help us stand up for what is right, even when it's hard. Amen.

Holy Places

Read Exodus 3:1-12
Or "Moses and the Special Holy Place" (*Story Bible*, pp. 90-91)

Close your eyes and think about a place where you feel safe, calm, and at peace. Maybe it's in your own bedroom, a quiet corner of your house, or a beautiful spot outside. Have you ever felt God there with you?

Some people call places where God feels extra close *thin places*, meaning that whatever sort of curtain or wall keeping us from seeing God all the time is extra thin in those places. Sometimes those places are out in nature, in a church building, or in another special, peaceful place. In the Bible, people often met God in the mountains, up and away from the crowded, busy places of ordinary life.

Moses met with God on mountains several times in the years when he was leading the Hebrew people out of slavery in Egypt to freedom in the promised land. The first time it happened, Moses was out tending sheep when he noticed a bush blazing with fire, which would catch anybody's attention! He quickly realized that this was no ordinary fire, however, since the leaves and branches of the bush were not burning away into ashes. God spoke to Moses out of the mysterious fire and told him to take off his shoes, because this place was holy.

Moses was shocked! He had never seen God like this before, but God had seen Moses and heard the cries of the Hebrew people suffering under Pharaoh. God wanted Moses to be the one to stand up to Pharaoh and deliver the people from slavery.

Not every encounter with God will be so powerful as Moses experienced, but God is still watching us and wants to be close to us. There is no rule about where you can feel close to God, but it often helps to get away from other people and noisy screens that might distract you. Find your own holy, thin place. Talk to God, and you may feel God talking back.

Discuss: What does it mean to see, hear, or feel God?

Discover: One famous thin place is Iona, an island off the coast of Scotland. Read about the Iona Community online.

Do: If you don't already have one, find or set up a place where you can feel at peace, where you can feel God with you.

Lord, help us quiet the noise around us so that we can hear your voice. Amen.

Let My People Go

Read Exodus 11; 12:21-36
Or "Terrible, Awful Times" (*Story Bible*, p. 92)

Moses was terrified to go back to Egypt and tell Pharaoh that God demanded he let the Hebrew people go. God had promised to go with Moses, though, and to show Pharaoh just how powerful God was. The seven chapters of Exodus 5 through 11 tell the long and sometimes scary story of an intense power struggle between Pharaoh and God. Over and over, Moses speaks God's message to Pharaoh: "Let my people go!"

Pharaoh didn't want to lose his workers, of course, so he decided to show Moses, God, and all the Hebrews who was in charge by making their work even longer and harder. God then showed them all who is even more powerful than Pharaoh. God sent ten plagues, tormenting Pharaoh and his people with frogs and flies, thunder and hail, blood in the water, and more. Pharaoh sometimes said "fine, go, just stop the plagues!" but he would quickly change his mind.

The final plague was the most serious, and God told Moses how to prepare the Hebrew people. Moses had the people ask Egyptians to give them silver and gold for their future life in freedom. He had the people make bread without yeast, so they wouldn't have to wait for dough to rise when they were fleeing the country. Finally, he had them paint lamb's blood on their doors as a sign so that the last plague—the plague of death—would pass over their houses.

After the plague of death killed the Egyptians' firstborn sons and livestock, Pharaoh finally gave up and sent the Hebrews away.

The story of how God rescued the people enslaved in Egypt is a central story for Jews and Christians alike. Jewish people still observe Passover as Exodus 12 instructed, and the phrase "remember you were once slaves in Egypt" is repeated throughout the Old Testament and in Passover prayers as a reminder of what God did for God's people and how we should have compassion for others who are oppressed. For Black Christians in the United States, the exodus story gave them hope during the horrible years of enslavement and is an ongoing reminder of how God wants people to be free.

> **Discuss:** How do you think Hebrew slaves felt while Moses and God fought Pharaoh for their freedom?
>
> **Discover:** Listen to a recording of the African American spiritual "Go Down Moses." Imagine how enslaved people felt singing this song.
>
> **Do:** Brainstorm together a list of people who are not free today—people in prison, people forced to work for very little or no pay, and more. Pray together for them.

Lord, this story has given hope to so many oppressed people, but it's also kind of scary. Help us remember that your greatest power—and ours—is love. Amen.

Trusting in Enough

Read Exodus 16:1-31
Or "Just Enough" (*Story Bible*, pp. 96-97)

When your youth group or sports team orders pizza for everybody, how many slices do you usually take? Three, because they might run out and not have enough for people to get seconds? Two, because that's how much usually fills you up? Or one, just in case there's not enough for everybody to have two?

It can be hard to know what's enough and to trust that there will be enough later, if you don't take it now.

The Hebrews were overjoyed to be free from slavery in Egypt, but their journey was far from over. They were traveling through a desert on foot, which can't be easy for anyone! (Good thing they didn't know yet that they would be traveling for forty years!) They often complained to Moses that there wasn't enough fresh water to drink or enough food to eat. Sometimes they would even say that slavery was better than the hardships they faced in the desert.

When the people complained how hungry they were, God sent quails every evening and manna every morning. Of course, some people tried to gather extra manna to save for the next day, worried that there wouldn't be enough in the future. The leftover manna turned wormy and gross overnight, though. The people had to learn to trust that there would be enough for every day and everyone, even on the day God asked them not to work.

For people who have experienced real hunger—not just a little stomach growling but rather uncertainty about when they will be able to eat again—taking enough for tomorrow and the next day, too, just makes sense. It takes time to trust that the pantry will still have food in it later.

People with plenty of food, money, or stuff have a different challenge when it comes to trust. They have to trust that they'll be OK with less, that having *just enough* is enough.

Discuss: What do we have enough of? Is there anything we *don't* have enough of?

Discover: Count how many food items are in your house right now. Share your best guesses beforehand and see who gets closest.

Do: If you have more than enough canned or boxed foods, unopened tubes of toothpaste, coats, or other things in your house, donate some to organizations that can connect them with people who do not have enough.

God, help us know what is enough so that there will be plenty for everyone who needs it. Amen.

Rules That Help Everyone

Read Exodus 20:1-21
Or "God Gives the Ten Commandments" (*Story Bible*, pp. 166-67)

When you were little, you may have followed rules just because a grown-up you trusted told you to. As you got a little older, though, "because I said so" probably seemed like a less convincing reason. You wanted to know *why* the rule was in place. As we grow, our minds and hearts are more able to understand how certain rules make life better for everyone.

Many people consider the Ten Commandments important just "because God said so," but when we spend more time with them, we realize that God's rules are designed to make life better for everyone. That was especially important because the Hebrews were just learning how to live together in community without Pharaoh and his taskmasters controlling their lives.

Some people say the first few commandments are about how we should relate to God (not worshiping anyone or anything other than God, for example) and the rest are about how we should relate to other people (like not killing people or stealing from them). Others say splitting the list in half like that misses something important about how loving God and loving other people are woven together. When we worship God, we learn to value all the people created in God's image. When we observe a Sabbath day each week, we remember what's really important in life—plus it's easier to be kind to

> **Sabbath** means rest, a time to stop working, renew our energy, and worship God.

others when we're well rested! When we respect other people and don't harm them with our words or actions, we embody God's love and desire for peace and justice.

Some rules we encounter can seem silly, outdated, or just plain unfair. Good rules help everybody live together safely and peacefully. When we're not sure what to do, looking to the Ten Commandments can help us make choices that honor God and other people.

Discuss: Which of the Ten Commandments do you find easiest and hardest to live by?

Discover: The Ten Commandments are repeated in Deuteronomy 5:6–21. Compare the two versions and see what you notice.

Do: Make a poster of the Ten Commandments for your house, with notes and drawings showing specific ideas for how your family can practice each one.

God, thank you for good rules that help us live together with kindness and peace. Amen.

No Fair!

Read Matthew 20:1-16
Or "The Generous Landowner" (*Story Bible*, pp. 226-27)

How do we know what's fair? Can you think of a situation that is definitely *not* fair?

Jesus told this parable about a situation that most people would think is not at all fair. A landowner needed many workers to tend his vineyard, and he hired more and more workers throughout the day. The workers the landowner hired early in the morning agreed to work all day for one coin. "That's fair," they said. They probably worked for more than twelve hours that day—their backs and hands were probably very sore. The ones hired later in the morning worked a pretty long time too, including during the hottest hours of the day.

The ones hired in the afternoon had an easier time. They were probably worried no one would hire them that day and were glad to get at least a half day's work. The ones hired in the evening may have been used to not getting hired. They probably got passed over for work because they looked less strong than other workers. Maybe they were old or had disabilities that made people think they wouldn't be good workers. They were probably thankful to be hired at all, even for just a little bit of work.

Imagine how excited the people who had worked all day must have been at first to see how generous the landowner was being. "Wow—if people who worked only a few hours are getting one coin, we must be getting a lot more!" They must have thought it was strange that the workers hired in the afternoon got the same amount as those hired in the evening. When they discovered that everybody was getting the same payment, whether they'd worked twelve hours or just two, they were furious! "No fair!" they cried.

Jesus said that God's kingdom was like this. Does that mean that God's not fair? Depends on what you think is fair. The landowner paid the workers who were there all day what they agreed was a fair wage, but he had a different idea of what would be fair to those who needed it most.

Discuss: Jesus ends the story by saying, "So the last will be first, and the first will be last" (v. 16). What do you think this means?

Discover: What is fair pay for a day's work where you live? Who decides what is fair?

Do: Prepare a container with small bills, snacks, and socks to keep in your car. When you encounter someone who needs money or can't find work, be generous—not because they've earned it but because they are in need.

Lord, when we are tempted to say something is not fair, help us look deeper and ask what we can do for other people, not what they can do for us. Amen.

Being Brave

Read Joshua 2:1-24
Or "Brave Rahab" (*Story Bible*, p. 76)

If any story in Scripture could be turned into an action movie, it should be this one. It has everything: an underdog army, spies and intrigue, and a brave and smart woman who knows what she wants.

Moses died before the Hebrews made it all the way to the promised land, which was known as the land of Canaan. A warrior named Joshua, who had led the Hebrews in battle against kings and armies they'd encountered on their journey, became the new leader. Joshua was preparing to lead the people across the river Jordan and into Canaan, so he sent two spies to scope out the city of Jericho.

The spies went directly to a house built into the city wall, one owned by a woman named Rahab. Rahab had heard about the Hebrews and how God had led them out of slavery and helped them in battle. The people of Canaan did not worship the God of the Hebrews, but like most ancient peoples, they believed that victory in battle meant the winning army's god was greater.

When the king of Jericho sent soldiers to Rahab's house looking for the spies, Rahab hid them and bravely told the soldiers they'd already left town. Only after the soldiers went away did she tell the spies what she knew about them and that, in return for protecting them, she wanted protection for her family when the Hebrew army attacked Jericho. Even though Rahab wasn't a Hebrew, the spies rescued her and her family as they said they would, and Rahab lived among the Hebrews for the rest of her life.

It must be pretty scary to know a battle is coming and to have soldiers knocking on your door. Rahab was probably pretty scared. But being brave doesn't mean being fearless. It means holding steady in the face of fear and doing what needs to be done even though you're scared. We often picture soldiers, maybe spies too, as brave. But the world is full of ordinary women like Rahab who face scary circumstances with bravery and brains. You probably know some! Think about their example when you need to be brave.

Discuss: Do you think God picks sides when armies fight?

Discover: This is the only story about Rahab in the Old Testament, but she is mentioned three times in the New Testament (Matt. 1:5, Heb. 11:31, and Jas. 2:25). Read about her legacy.

Do: Get some red string or cord like Rahab hung in her window. Tie a knot in it for every brave woman you can think of. Give thanks for the smart and courageous women in your church and community.

God, thank you for brave women like Rahab and [insert names of brave women you know]. Amen.

Choosing God

Read Joshua 24:1-24
Or "Remember, Choose, Serve" (*Story Bible*, pp. 104-5)

Do you remember the first time you went to church? How old were you? Did your family take you, or did you go with a friend?

Most people who are part of a religious tradition—who think about and worship God in a particular way—learn it from their families. Beliefs and ideas get passed down from generation to generation as grown-ups teach children the stories and traditions of their faith. Even when you've been a part of something your whole life, though, there comes a time when you have to make choices about it for yourself.

Toward the end of his life, the Hebrew leader Joshua gave a passionate speech to the people reminding them of all that God had done for them. He started all the way back with their ancestor Abraham and the story of how God led Abraham and Sarah to a new place in Canaan, far away from their families and the other gods they had worshiped. Joshua told the whole, long story of how Abraham's great-grandchildren ended up in Egypt and how God led them out of Egypt, through the wilderness for many years, and finally back to Canaan.

> **Tradition** is a belief or action that is passed from generation to generation in a family or culture.

Even after saying how their ancestors had followed God for so many years, Joshua told the people they had to choose whether they would keep following.

The choice to follow and serve God is a big one—and it's one you make over and over again. As you grow and get to know God more and more, you choose. When life gets confusing and scary, you choose. When you grow up and make your own family, you choose. Every choice might look a little different, because you'll be different. Your journey with God might look different from your family members', but God will be there every step of the way.

Discuss: What choices have you made in your journey with God?

Discover: Are there any special objects in your house that symbolize your family's journey with God?

Do: Write down creative ideas for serving God together as a family. Put them on popsicle sticks or slips of paper and pick out one each week to try.

God, you are so faithful to us. Thank you for the opportunity to journey with you all our lives. Amen.

Friends Who Help

Read Job 4:1-9; 6:1-4, 14-17
Or "God Remembers Job" (*Story Bible*, pp. 122-23)

The book of Job begins, "There once was a man . . ." If that reminds you a little of "once upon a time," you would be onto something. Like a fable or parable, this story of a man's extreme suffering is told and retold because people are always trying to figure out why bad things happen and how to respond when they do.

Our human sense of justice says that good things should happen to good people and bad things should happen only to bad people, but we know from experience that that isn't how things work. For one thing, no one is all good or all bad, and the things that happen to us in life are generally unrelated to our level of goodness.

When we get sick or suffer a disaster of some kind, we need the support of our loved ones, not their theories on why diseases and disasters happen. We need caring words and kind gestures, like bringing a meal or helping clean up, or even just sitting and listening. Good friends focus on making things better.

Rather than comforting Job, Job's friends were more concerned with trying to make it all make sense. Job's friends were insistent that since God is fair, Job must have deserved the things that were happening to him. "You must have done something!" they said. Job insisted that he had done nothing wrong, but his friends refused to believe him. If they could convince themselves that bad things happen only to people who have done something bad, they might feel safer and more confident that nothing bad would happen to them.

At the end of the story, God says we're never going to understand everything that happens in the world and that Job's friends were wrong to claim they did.

We want the world to make sense, and sometimes it just doesn't. But if we focus on caring for one another, we will all get through life's hard times with a little less damage and a lot more love.

Discuss: How can we be good friends to someone having a hard time?

Discover: Research what kinds of donations help people after a disaster and what kinds of donations make things harder.

Do: Think about a group of people who are struggling right now in your community, state, or elsewhere. Write a letter to your city council or state representative to advocate for bills or programs that could help them.

God, help us be good friends to people struggling with hard times. Amen.

Chosen Family

Read Ruth 1:1-19a
Or "Leaving Moab" (*Story Bible*, pp. 60-61)

Ruth is one of only two women to have a book of the Bible named for them. (Esther is the other.) Her story is best known for the words she said to Naomi, promising to never leave her: "Where you go, I will go; where you lodge, I will lodge; your people shall be my people and your God my God" (v. 16).

People often read those words at weddings, because the promise to stay together forever sounds like the promises that people make when they get married. Ruth and Orpah might have made promises like those to Naomi's sons when they got married.

In those times, women went and lived with their husband's family when they got married and took care of their husband's parents when they got old. When all the men in the family died, Ruth and Naomi weren't officially family anymore. Naomi told Ruth and Orpah that they should go back to their own families, who lived far away. Orpah reluctantly left, but Ruth refused. Whether or not they were officially family, Ruth chose Naomi as her family, no matter what the future would bring.

Many people today have what they call *chosen family*—friends, neighbors, and others whom they feel close to, support and rely on, and celebrate life events with. For some people, chosen family takes the place of official family when family members die, live far away, or aren't able to provide the love and support family members should. For others, chosen family is a special bonus in addition to biological family, an extra group of people to love and support one another.

We may have to make more of an effort to talk to and be there for the people we love when they don't live in our house. But those relationships are important and worth committing ourselves to.

> **Discuss:** Are there people in your life who are like family to you, even though they aren't related to you?
>
> **Discover:** Read the rest of Ruth's story. How do Ruth and Naomi help each other?
>
> **Do:** Make plans to connect more with special people outside your family. Maybe invite another family over for dinner or do a video call with friends who live far away.

Lord, thank you for our family and for friends who feel like family. Amen.

No King, Just God

Read 1 Samuel 8:1-22
Or "Samuel Finds a New King" (*Story Bible*, pp. 108-9)

When thinking about kings, you might picture a king in a fairy tale—a bearded guy with a crown who mainly tries to keep his daughter, the princess, from doing what she wants. Or maybe you think about the king of England or another modern-day royal who attends ceremonies and looks fancy but doesn't have a lot of real power.

Kings in ancient times (and times not too far back from our own!) could be a lot more dangerous. For a while after the Hebrews settled in Canaan, wise judges and faithful priests led the people in different ways when needed, but they didn't have a king like the other nations around them. People considered kings to be like gods, and God's first commandment had been not to treat anybody or anything else like God. But things got hard. The judges weren't as wise and the priests weren't as faithful, so the people started to think it would be better to have a king.

They turned to Samuel, a prophet who had been hearing from and talking to God since he was a little boy. They asked him to find a king for their people. Samuel knew that was a bad idea and asked God what he should do. God said, "They have rejected me. Give them what they want, but warn them what a king will do."

So Samuel told the people how kings have power to make people do whatever he wants, forcing them to be soldiers or slaves, taking their land and property to be his own, and not treating them fairly. But the people still wanted a king.

They became the kingdom of Israel and had kings rule over them for the next few centuries. Just as Samuel had warned them, many of the kings were selfish and didn't listen to God. Having a lot of power sometimes makes a person think that they are like God. We must remember that only God is God.

> **Prophets** were people called by God to deliver important messages from God to the people.

Discuss: What would you do if you had the power to rule over everybody else in your house? What would keep you from abusing your power?

Discover: Jesus talked a lot about the kingdom of God or the kingdom of heaven. What did Jesus say a world with God in charge would be like?

Do: Make a crown out of paper and craft supplies. Put it somewhere you will see it and remember that God is the only one worthy of power and praise.

Lord, give our leaders humility and wisdom, and help us all remember that only you are God. Amen.

God Looks at the Heart

Read 1 Samuel 16:1-13
Or "A Brand-New King" (*Story Bible*, pp. 110-11)

Here's a fun fact: almost all U.S. presidents have been taller than the average man in their time. There's no evidence that being tall makes you a better leader, but we often assume they are. People tend to vote for taller candidates.

Israel's first king was a tall and handsome man named Saul. People thought he looked as if he'd be a good, strong leader, but it turned out that he wasn't. God and the prophet Samuel were both very disappointed. God told Samuel to anoint someone new to be king, even though Saul was still alive!

So God sent Samuel to Bethlehem, to the family of a man named Jesse. "One of Jesse's sons will be the next king," God said. "I'll tell you which one when you see him."

It took Samuel a while to find the one

God had chosen, because Samuel was still assuming that taller and stronger-looking people, such as Jesse's older sons, make better leaders. Samuel must have forgotten about the Hebrew ancestors Jacob and Joseph—younger sons whom God nonetheless chose as important leaders. God reminded Samuel that "the Lord does not see as mortals see; they look on the outward appearance, but the Lord looks on the heart" (v. 7).

So Samuel asked if Jesse had any other sons. Jesse hadn't even bothered to bring his youngest son along on the day's outing! That son, David, was out tending his father's sheep. He came in from the field, and Samuel knew that David was the one God had chosen.

Years passed before Saul died and David became king, but God saw that David had a good heart and could make a very good king. David also made some selfish choices and hurtful mistakes when he was king, but he kept trying to follow God, no matter what.

> **Discuss:** Do you ever judge people based on how they look? How can you look at their heart instead?
>
> **Discover:** Find a book or video about Malala Yousafzai, Greta Thunberg, or someone else who became a leader at a young age.
>
> **Do:** Cut out a large paper heart and decorate it with a list of qualities God looks for in a great leader.

God, help us see other people and ourselves as you see us, looking at what's in our hearts. Amen.

A Good Neighbor

Read Luke 10:25-37
Or "The Good Neighbor" (*Story Bible*, pp. 212-13)

Sometimes we call someone who does a good deed "a good Samaritan." What does that mean? What even is a Samaritan?

Samaritans were a group of people whom many Jews in Jesus' time considered their enemies. When Jesus made a Samaritan the hero of his story, that was a surprising twist.

Jesus often made people uncomfortable, challenging their ways of thinking and living. So, certain people were always trying to trip up Jesus, to see if he was really a good Jew or if his ideas were just too out there to accept. The man who asked Jesus, "And who is my neighbor?" might have called Jesus crazy if Jesus had replied, "Everybody—even Samaritans!" So Jesus used a story to help the man answer his own question.

In this parable, a man was injured by robbers. Two people whom everyone listening would have expected to be kind and offer help didn't, but someone whom they considered an outsider, not a neighbor, did stop and help! Not only that, but he took the man to an inn where he could recover and paid the innkeeper to look after him!

"Which person was a neighbor to the injured man?" Jesus asked the man who was questioning him.

"The one who showed kindness," he replied.

Jesus helped the man see that loving your neighbor means being kind and caring for anyone who needs it, no matter who they are. That's the kind of neighbor God wants us to be.

> **Discuss:** Are there any groups of people today whom many people distrust and would be surprised to see held up as a model of kindness? Or that you might hesitate to help?
>
> **Discover:** Do some research to find out where the differences between Jews and Samaritans began.
>
> **Do:** Act out the story. How does it feel to play each part?

God, help us see all people as our neighbors and show kindness to our enemies as well as our friends. Amen.

Where God Lives

Read 2 Samuel 7:1-9
Or "Taking Special Care" and "Solomon Builds the Temple"
(*Story Bible*, pp. 114-15 and 126-27)

Where does God live? Some people picture God living on fluffy clouds or on a shining, heavenly throne. Maybe we picture the universe and imagine God being somewhere out there, far away from earth. Or maybe you think of God hanging out in your church, waiting for you to come visit.

The ancient Hebrews saw God as traveling along with them, hovering around the special golden chest they'd built to hold the stone tablets with the Ten Commandments written on them. They carried this chest, called the ark of the covenant, with them on their journey to the promised land, and King David brought it to his capital city of Jerusalem.

David had prepared a tent to place the chest in but soon wondered if it was wrong for God to live in a tent while the king lived in a sturdy house. God responded to David, saying, "I've been with my people wherever they've been, and I've been with you since you were a little boy tending sheep in a field. Have I ever said I need a house to live in?"

In other words, "Thanks but no thanks!"

God said that one of David's sons could build a house for God. Years later, David's son King Solomon built an amazing temple for God with gold and bronze, precious gemstones, and ornate carvings. There was space for the people to worship God and a special room to hold the ark of the covenant.

God was there in the temple, just as God is in the houses of worship we build today—churches and mosques, synagogues and temples and gurdwaras. But God isn't just in those places. God is everywhere. God is in each of us. If you feel as if God is hard to find, just remember that God is love, and wherever love is, there is God. Love yourself and others well, and you will find God there.

Discuss: How do you picture God? Where is God in your vision?

Discover: Look up images showing what the ark of the covenant and the temple in Jerusalem might have looked like.

Do: Visit God in a new place—a stream or forest you've never explored, or a different house of worship. On your way there, talk about how God is already there. On the way home, share how you saw God in that new place.

God, it is so amazing that you can be everywhere in the universe and also right here with us. Amen.

Telling Hard Truths

Read Amos 5:10-24
Or "Telling the Truth" (*Story Bible*, pp. 142-43)

Even though God was with the people no matter what, God's people often forgot the covenant God had made with them. They forgot that God was their God, and they didn't follow God's ways. When that happened, God chose a prophet to speak words from God to God's people.

It was a prophet's job to tell hard truths. They called out people on their behavior and warned them that if they didn't change their ways—treat people fairly and kindly, quit worshiping idols and turn to God—then things wouldn't go well for them.

Amos was one of God's prophets. He believed wholeheartedly in God's message of justice and compassion and preached that message fiercely. Amos saw how badly poor people were being treated in Israel and called out the rich and powerful people who ignored or took advantage of them. Amos spoke for God, saying that the people's worship and offerings meant nothing if they weren't treating people with kindness and dignity.

> **Justice** means making things right, good, or fair.

God still calls prophets to speak out against injustice. Martin Luther King Jr. spoke out against racial and economic inequality in the mid-twentieth century, even quoting Amos 5:24 in one of his famous speeches: "Let justice roll down like water and righteousness like an ever-flowing stream."

When you see people being treated unfairly, you can speak out too. If someone is bullying others at school or talking about others in a demeaning way (even if their target isn't around to hear it), speak up! If leaders are making laws that make life harder for people who are already struggling, speak up! People may not like hearing hard truths about how their actions are hurting other people, but if we stay quiet, nothing will change. This is the hard work of a prophet.

Discuss: Who are prophets today who remind us about how we are to live in community and care for all people? How can we follow their example?

Discover: Look in your Bible's table of contents. Does it label certain books as being by or about prophets? Which books are included in that list?

Do: Talk about people who are being hurt or taken advantage of in your school or community. Write a letter or email to someone in charge about correcting the injustice.

God, thank you for prophets who remind us what is good and right, even when we don't want to hear it. Amen.

The Pouting Prophet

Read Jonah 3:1-5; 4:1-11
Or "Jonah Runs Away" and "A Second Chance for Jonah"
(*Story Bible*, pp. 132-35)

Nobody likes to be scolded. That's why prophets sometimes got run out of town or were just plain ignored, despite their good intentions to guide people back to God. Prophets like Amos, Jeremiah, Hosea, and others would plead with the people and then lament when the people refused to listen.

The prophet Jonah's story is different, so much that it's even kind of funny. God wanted Jonah to go preach to the Ninevites and tell them to change their ways. Jonah didn't want to—Nineveh was Israel's enemy—and instead boarded a boat headed in the opposite direction. You've probably heard this part of the story before, where Jonah got thrown overboard and God sent a big fish to save him.

Given a second chance to do what God said, Jonah reluctantly went to Nineveh and half-heartedly told the people to quit their evil ways or God would destroy their city. You can almost imagine Jonah mumbling his message at double speed, barely caring if anyone could hear or understand him! But that's when the story really gets crazy. Rather than getting mad at Jonah or rolling their eyes, the Ninevites actually repented, from the king down to the farm animals. And rather than rejoicing that his preaching worked and that the city was saved, Jonah got mad at God!

"See? This is why I didn't want to go!" Jonah cried. "I knew you were a loving God and wouldn't actually punish those horrible Ninevites!" He stormed off to pout, even throwing a fit about a shade tree.

Jonah just might be the most relatable prophet. He knows he's being petty and irrational, but he makes a big show of being angry anyway. Jonah's story is a great reminder that God cares for everyone—even when we don't.

Like Jonah, we sometimes think God dislikes the same people we dislike. We might want God to punish those people, but that's not how God works. There's no bigger challenge than to try to love others as much as God does.

Discuss: Would you have acted as Jonah did in his situation? Why or why not?

Discover: Look up Nineveh and Tarshish on a map.

Do: Act out the part of the story after Nineveh is saved (Jonah 4:1–11).

We know you are a loving God—and that's a good thing! Help us love even our enemies the way you do. Amen.

God Is with Us

Read Isaiah 7:10-16; 9:2-7; 43:1-7
Or "You Are Not Alone" (*Story Bible*, pp. 146-47)

Think about a time when you were really scared. Did you feel alone? Did it help to have someone with you when you were scared, to let you know you weren't alone in facing your fears?

The prophet Isaiah spoke and wrote to people who were really scared. Their world seemed to be falling apart. The kingdom of Israel that David and Solomon had ruled over had split, dividing into the Northern Kingdom still called Israel and the Southern Kingdom called Judah. Armies were threatening to attack both kingdoms. Israel was defeated and then Judah. The Babylonian army destroyed the beautiful temple in Jerusalem and took many people back to Babylon with them, to keep them from rebuilding their city.

Amid all that terror, Isaiah gave warnings (as prophets do) but also gave the people hope, telling them that God was with them.

To a king afraid of invaders, Isaiah used the image of a baby named Immanuel, meaning "God with us." Before that baby is even old enough to know right from wrong, Isaiah said, the armies threatening Judah will fall apart. So don't be afraid—God is with us.

To the people who were afraid that war would soon come to their land, Isaiah said that one day there would be peace—peace so complete that they could get rid of their soldiers' boots and uniforms—and a king would reign who was more wonderful, just, and righteous than any who came before. He would be a prince of peace! So don't be afraid—God is with us.

To the people exiled in Babylon, held captive, and afraid they would never see their homeland again, Isaiah gave a message direct from God: "I created you, I know you, and I love you. Don't be afraid—I am with you."

You might have scary times in your life. You might be really, really afraid. No matter what, God is with you.

Discuss: How can remembering that God is with you help when you are afraid? How can we help others be less afraid?

Discover: See what you can learn about the Babylonian exile. What would it be like to be forcibly removed from your home?

Do: Make a sign using Isaiah's comforting words to remind you that God is always with you.

Lord, you have created us, formed us, and called us by name. We are yours. Amen.

What Mary Knew

Read Luke 1:26-56
Or "How Can This Happen?" (*Story Bible*, p. 186)

How would you react if an angel showed up in your house right now? Can you imagine being Mary when the angel appeared to her and said she would have a baby through the Holy Spirit?

Mary was most likely a young teenager, maybe only thirteen or fourteen years old. The Gospel writer Luke says that she was engaged but not yet married. Young girls in this time in history without power or much money would not have been listened to or respected. If Joseph refused to believe her story about the angel, he might have left her, and her parents might not have found anyone else to marry her. Her life could have been ruined.

> The New Testament begins with four books about Jesus' life: Matthew, Mark, Luke, and John. We call these the Gospels. **Gospel** means "good news" and is also used to describe Jesus' overall message.

Why would God choose Mary for this important job? Why would God ask her to take such a huge risk? And why would she say yes?

If we've been paying attention, it shouldn't surprise us that God chose someone the world would consider small and unimportant to do something big and very important. From younger brother Jacob to little David who became king, God loves flipping our expectations upside down. If God had chosen a rich woman or princess to carry God's son, the world would go right on thinking that only those people matter. God wanted everyone to know that no one is unimportant to God.

Mary knew that God was with people like her. That's how she had the confidence to say yes to the angel's strange request. God would be with her, and God can do anything! "God will do amazing things through me and this baby," Mary said. "God will turn the world upside down, lifting up the lowly and showing the powerful how powerless they really are. The hungry will have plenty to eat and everyone will see how merciful and strong God is!"

If you ever feel too young or powerless to do something important, remember Mary and what Mary knew about God: God loves using unexpected heroes to turn the world upside down.

> **Discuss:** What would the world look like if rich and powerful people switched places with the poorest people and if those who are currently overlooked were in charge?
>
> **Discover:** Ask the grown-ups in the room how they felt when they found out each child would join the family.
>
> **Do:** Help moms living in poverty get ready for their babies by collecting items for a shelter or community baby shower.

God, we know you can use anyone to bring your love to the world. Use us to do something big! Amen.

An Ordinary, Extraordinary Baby

Read Luke 2:1-7
Or "A Baby Is Born" (*Story Bible*, pp. 190-91)

At Christmastime, our houses often look the fanciest they do all year, with lights and shiny gold ornaments. We might get things ready for guests to visit, cleaning the house and putting fresh sheets on the guest bed. We enjoy special food and might even dress up for the occasion. This all seems fitting for celebrating Jesus' birth, because Jesus is so special. He's called the King of Kings, the Lord of Lords, the Prince of Peace, after all.

Jesus' birth was about as different from this festive scene as you can imagine. Rather than clean sheets and sparkling windows, Mary and Joseph had to stay in the dirty, dark bottom floor of the house. Not where guests would stay, but where animals lived. There were no fancy foods or clothes, just the same boring basics a poor family might use every day.

This is not what you would plan or expect for a king or a prince, but it's exactly what God wanted. God wanted their son to live like an ordinary human. There were no hospitals back then, so babies were born at home or—if the parents were traveling like Mary and Joseph—any place they could find. If God's son was an ordinary person, people would know that God could understand their lives as ordinary people and care about the ordinary things they do.

The prophet Isaiah talked about a child who would be called Immanuel, which means "God with us." Jesus was born to be

God with us—God living life here on earth like us and in relationship with us ordinary people. Isn't that extraordinary?

Discuss: If Jesus were to be born today like an ordinary baby, what would his life be like?

Discover: How many pictures or statues of Jesus do you have in your house? Do they make Jesus look ordinary or extra special?

Do: Find two small sticks and place them in a cross formation. Using instructions that can be found online, wrap the sticks in yarn to make a God's Eye craft. Think of the cross symbolizing Jesus and how he lived as God's eyes, ears, hands, and feet on earth.

God, thank you for being with us on earth. It's so amazing that Jesus was born like an ordinary baby to experience life as we do. Amen.

Visitors from Near and Far

Read Luke 2:8-20; Matthew 2:1-12
Or "Surprise Visitors" and "Visitors from the East"
(*Story Bible*, pp. 192-93 and 196-97)

Christmas plays and pictures imagining Jesus' birth often show the shepherds and magi (who we often call wise men) all together around the manger, but the stories of each group's visit to see Jesus aren't even in the same book of the Bible!

Luke tells the story of shepherds guarding their sheep in a field on the very night Jesus was born. An angel tells them to go to Bethlehem and see the Messiah, who has just been born in Bethlehem, the same town in which the great King David had been born.

Matthew, on the other hand, tells the story of magi from the East who saw a new star in the sky, meaning that a new king had been born. They traveled for months or even years before they arrived in Jerusalem to ask King Herod about a new king of the Jews. Herod was upset that someone else might be called king but knew these astrologers from far away must be talking about the Messiah.

Matthew and Luke are two of the four Gospels included in our Bible. Different writers included different stories about Jesus to tell us what they thought was most important and what they most wanted the people who would read their writings to know. The stories of the shepherds and the magi both show

> **Messiah** means "anointed one" and refers especially to an anticipated descendant of King David who would come to save Israel.

us how holy and significant Jesus' birth was. They both say that Jesus was the Messiah and was born in Bethlehem—showing that Jesus was an important leader like King David. The story of the shepherds shows us how Jesus' birth was important for everyone, including ordinary people like shepherds. The story of the magi shows us how Jesus' birth was important for everyone, including people who lived far away and didn't already worship God.

Near and far, rich and poor, Jesus is here for everyone.

Discuss: If you were writing a book about your family, what stories would you include? What would you include if you were writing a book about Jesus' family?

Discover: Some traditions suggest that the magi were from Persia (modern-day Iran), Arabia, India, or even China. Look at a map to see where those countries are in relation to Bethlehem. What geographical features, like mountains, deserts, or rivers, might have made traveling through these areas difficult for the magi?

Do: Act out the story of Jesus' birth. What characters will you include?

Lord, help us share the good news of Jesus' message with people far and near. Amen.

Learning from One Another

Read Luke 2:39-52
Or "When Jesus Was Twelve" (*Story Bible*, pp. 198-99)

Years ago, people used to say things like, "Children should be seen and not heard," and "Don't speak unless you're spoken to." Adults didn't want to hear what kids thought about things, especially if the grown-ups hadn't asked for the child's input. Today, many adults want to hear what kids have to say, but they might still be surprised if someone a lot younger than them seems to be smarter or know more about something than they do.

All the adults in today's story were surprised by twelve-year-old Jesus. Mary and Joseph were shocked to realize that their son wasn't anywhere in the large group they were traveling with, and they were very anxious as they looked for him in Jerusalem for three days. They finally found him in the temple, where the teachers were amazed at Jesus' questions and answers.

The teachers were adult men who had spent many years studying Scripture, but even at a young age, Jesus was able to ask insightful questions and talk about God in ways that surprised the men. (Women weren't allowed to be teachers or go to school back then, so imagine how shocked they would have been if Jesus had been a girl!) Jesus perplexed them all with his response to their astonishment: "Did you not know I must be in my Father's house?" (v. 49).

Jesus may have understood things about God that even those grown men did not, but he still asked questions. He and the teachers learned from one another. Asking questions and talking with others about God is a great way to grow in our faith. We all have different experiences, ideas, and perspectives. We can learn from one another and be inspired to keep thinking about things for ourselves. None of us have all the answers, and there's always more to discover.

Discuss: Outside of your home, where is a place you interact with people much older or younger than you? What is something you've learned from someone of a different generation?

Discover: What are some ways parents and kids can keep from getting separated in public places?

Do: Take turns teaching the rest of the family something you've learned recently. The person closest to age twelve goes first!

God, you are so amazing. We want to know you more and more. Amen.

Jesus Is Baptized

Read Matthew 3:1-17
Or "An Awesome Day" (*Story Bible*, p. 202)

Have you seen any of the movies in which a kid goes to sleep one night and wakes up as an adult? Jesus' story seems kind of like that—not because he magically skipped all those years but because the Bible doesn't include any stories about Jesus from age thirteen to around thirty!

We first see adult Jesus when he goes to be baptized by his cousin, John. John was a prophet who reminded people a lot of the prophets from centuries before. He dressed like the prophet Elijah and quoted the prophet Isaiah, saying "Prepare the way of the Lord!" (v. 3).

Similar to the prophets of old, he had a serious message for the people: "Repent! Change your ways!" John baptized people to symbolize their repentance, washing away sin so that they could have a fresh start.

> **Repentance** means turning around and changing your ways to be more faithful to God.

People wondered if John could be Elijah back from the dead or the Messiah, but John told them to keep looking, keep getting ready. Someone else was coming with an even more powerful message. Someone else would baptize them not with water but with the Holy Spirit and fire, not just washing away but burning away their sin forever.

It makes sense that when Jesus came to John and asked to be baptized, John wanted to refuse. Why would Jesus need to repent? People still talk about why Jesus wanted to be baptized. We don't know if Jesus saw his baptism as a fresh start, but it was definitely the start of something. God's voice announced to everyone that Jesus was God's beloved child, and from there Jesus set out on a mission to teach and heal and change the world.

If you've been baptized, that was the start of something too. Some people are baptized as babies, symbolizing how we are children of God from the very start of our lives. Some people are baptized after being part of a church and following God for years; their baptism marks the start of a new chapter in their faith. Some people are baptized after meeting God as adults. No matter when—or if—you were baptized, every day can be a fresh start with God.

Discuss: Why do you think Jesus wanted to be baptized? Would you have wanted to be baptized by John?

Discover: All four Gospels tell this story. Read them all and compare the details: Matthew 3:1–17, Mark 1:1–11, Luke 3:1–22, and John 1:19–34.

Do: Share pictures and stories of the baptisms in your family. Mark the days they happened on the family calendar and celebrate those anniversaries each year.

Lord, help us turn away from sinful things and toward you. Give us a fresh start every day. Amen.

It's Very Tempting

Read Luke 4:1-12
Or "A Wild Test" (*Story Bible*, pp. 204-5)

Do you ever feel tempted to do something you know you shouldn't? Whether it's a split-second decision to say something that might hurt someone or an agonizing struggle to make the right decision, temptation can be hard. Like in cartoons where someone has an angel on one shoulder and a devil on the other, we might argue within ourselves before resisting temptation or giving in.

When Jesus was tempted in the wilderness, he seemed to have quick answers to the devil's temptations. Turn rocks into bread? *No, I'm hungry, but I need God more.* Worship the devil and become king of the world? *No, I worship only God.*

Jesus didn't use his own words, though. He quoted Scripture to explain to the devil (or maybe remind himself) why he shouldn't do what the devil was suggesting. So the devil quoted Scripture back at Jesus, telling Jesus to jump off the temple because Psalm 91 says God would send angels to catch him. Jesus didn't take the bait, though. He quoted Moses, saying, "Do not put the Lord your God to the test" (v. 12).

Sometimes, we'll find any excuse to do what we really want to do, even if we know it's wrong. The devil showed how easy it is to use even the Bible to make such excuses. The Bible is so big and diverse, you can find a verse of Scripture for just about anything you want to argue. People have used the Bible to argue both for and against slavery, segregation, immigration, and even feeding someone who is begging for food!

Jesus could have said, "Moses tapped a rock and made water come out, so I can tap a rock to make bread." Instead, he trusted God. Jesus knew Scripture, but what matters more is that he knew God, so he knew in his heart what to do. The Bible isn't meant to be a grab bag of sayings to pull from when you need to prove a point but a resource to get to know God better. Study Scripture, pray, and think about how your actions affect others. Then you'll know in your heart what God wants you to do.

Discuss: How can God help us make good decisions?

Discover: Some Christians observe Lent, forty days of spiritual preparation inspired by Jesus' forty days in the wilderness. Research the traditions and practices of Lent.

Do: Paint rocks with encouraging words and pictures. Place them outside so that others can be nourished by them.

God, speak to our hearts and help us do the right thing—even when it's really hard. Amen.

Drop Everything

Read Matthew 4:18-22; 10:1-4
Or "Follow Me!" (*Story Bible*, p. 206)

Imagine the most ordinary day. You're on your way to school or at your job, or maybe just relaxing at home. Jesus walks by and asks you to follow him. Leave behind whatever you were doing that day or planning to do for the next few years of your life and go. No, it's not a paying gig. Some meals might be provided, but we don't know for sure. Oh, and we're walking. Be sure to bring your good sandals.

Would you go? What would your parents or friends say?

It's pretty shocking that Jesus convinced twelve people to give up everything and travel with him, helping and learning as he taught and healed people all over the region. Peter, Andrew, James, and John were all fishermen, hauling in their daily catch, mending nets that had been torn—and they simply dropped their nets and followed, leaving their family businesses in a lurch.

Another disciple, Matthew, was a tax collector. Tax collectors took money from the Jewish people on behalf of the powerful Roman Empire, which ruled over the whole region. These local tax collectors could collect extra money for their pay, so their fellow Jews often saw them as greedy traitors. When Jesus called Matthew (9:9), the tax collector got up and followed, no questions asked, even though it meant losing money and hanging out with people who might not like him very much!

> A **disciple** is someone who closely follows and learns from their teacher.

Jesus called twelve disciples to be his closest followers and friends. He taught them and empowered them to go out themselves and heal people. He also warned them of how some people might not welcome them and might even try to harm them. They were giving up their safety as well as their home and livelihood! When the twelve disciples dropped everything to follow Jesus, they were taking a big risk. What would their future hold?

Discuss: What could have been so compelling about Jesus that people would leave their jobs and families to follow him? Would leaving everything be easier for some people than others? Why?

Discover: There is a famous book titled *The Cost of Discipleship* by Dietrich Bonhoeffer. Search online to learn about Bonhoeffer's remarkable life.

Do: Write a list of things you've learned from Jesus. You're a disciple too!

Lord, you call us to follow you every day. Give us the strength to be your disciples. Amen.

Living Water

Read John 4:1-30
Or "The Very Thirsty Woman" (*Story Bible*, p. 236)

Water is essential for life. You probably know that. Humans, other animals, and plants cannot survive without enough water. Water is so important to our physical life that Jesus used it to describe something else that is essential: the spiritual life that is found in God.

Jesus and his disciples were traveling, and while they  usually visited areas where their fellow Jews lived, sometimes they traveled through other areas. They were taking a shortcut through Samaria. Remember the story of "The Good Neighbor" (p. 58) in which we learned that Samaritans and Jews did not like each other. Both groups were descended from Jacob's twelve sons, but Samaritans worshiped God on a mountain in their land while Jews made the temple in Jerusalem the center of their worship. This disagreement had divided them for hundreds of years.

Jesus surprised his disciples by getting into a conversation with someone there that was both a Samaritan and a woman! Samaritan or not, women were generally considered less important than men and not worthy of public consideration. Jesus was crossing boundaries of both ethnicity and gender!

The woman herself was shocked that Jesus was talking to her and even asking to drink water from her bucket at the well. Jesus surprised her further by saying he could give her "living water," water you don't have to draw from a well but that springs up like a fountain leading to eternal life.

Still, the woman questioned why he would offer her such a gift, given their differences. Jesus explained that soon, it wouldn't matter *where* you were physically when you worshiped God. What matters is that you worship in your spirit, flowing with living water.

> **Discuss:** How would you have felt if you were the woman talking with Jesus at the well?
>
> **Discover:** Find a map showing Judea and Samaria in the first century. There might be one in your Bible. What names of cities and towns do you recognize from stories about Jesus?
>
> **Do:** Prepare a box of water bottles to keep in your car and hand out to people in need of a cool drink.

Lord, refresh us with living water so that we can experience thriving, eternal life with you. Amen.

Jesus Heals

Read John 4:46-54
Or "Jesus Heals with Words" (*Story Bible*, pp. 254-55)

The Bible has a lot of stories about people who were healed or miracles that happened, both in the Old Testament and New Testament. When you read them, it makes you pause and think: Do these kinds of things still happen today? You may have prayed for God to heal a loved one of illness, but they died anyway. It's hard to know why some people recover and some people don't.

All kinds of differently abled people came to Jesus. They wanted to touch him. They wanted his healing presence. Women who were ill, men who couldn't walk, parents who wanted healing for a child who was sick, a man who was blind and wanted to see: they all sought Jesus' healing help. They all came to him believing that with his help, they could be healed. They came with their bodies as they were, and they also came with faith and hope in how Jesus could help them.

One man Jesus met had traveled a whole day's journey to ask Jesus to come heal his sick son. The man begged Jesus to walk back with him so that he could physically see and touch the boy. Rather than traveling that long distance and making a dramatic scene that would get bystanders excited, Jesus simply assured the father with his words that the boy would recover. When he got home, the man was shocked to find that his son was alive and that his condition had begun to improve right around the time Jesus had spoken those words so far away. Jesus had healed the boy without even seeing him.

Miraculous healings still happen today, but maybe in ways that are different from the times when Jesus lived. Medicines and treatments could be considered miracles. People also find healing through faith and love and friendship, feeling at peace whether or not their disease is cured. Most of us can't cure someone through our touch, but we can use words to help people who are sick or suffering. Speaking or writing messages of hope and love can be a soothing balm for someone in pain, even when you are far away.

Discuss: How is being healed different from being cured?

Discover: Count how many medicines you have in your house. When you are sick, is it a medicine that helps you the most or something else?

Do: Make cards to deliver to a local hospital or nursing home. The staff will know who most needs the boost your caring words can offer.

God, we don't know why some people are cured and others aren't. Empower us to heal hearts with loving words and actions. Amen.

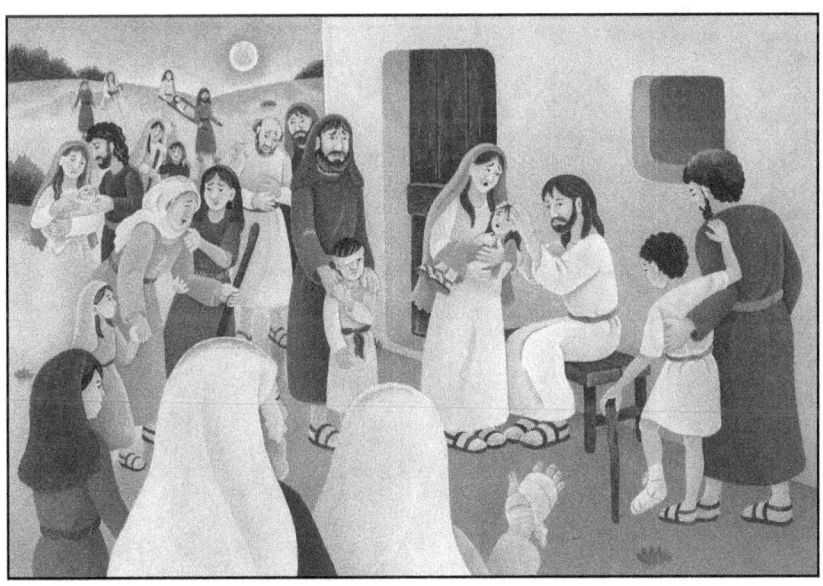

Everybody Counts

Read Luke 15:1-32
Or "Two Sons and Their Father" (*Story Bible*, pp. 218-19)

Have you ever been teased or criticized for who you hang out with? Maybe you have a friend who's considered uncool or different in some way. Some of the religious leaders in Jesus' time said Jesus must not be very holy because he spent time with tax collectors and sinners. We don't know what those people's sins were, but for whatever reason, the religious leaders saw them as lost, far away from God.

In response, Jesus told them three stories about lost things. There was a shepherd with a hundred sheep, and he risked something happening to ninety-nine of them in order to search for and bring back the one sheep that had wandered away and

gotten lost. There was a woman who cleaned her house from top to bottom to find one silver coin that had gone missing—even though she still had nine other coins. There was a man with two sons; the younger one ran off and wasted his dad's money, but the dad still threw a big party when he came back home.

Every person matters, Jesus was saying. Everybody counts! Even these people you call sinners. God's family isn't complete if even one person is missing.

This was good news to the people Jesus was hanging out with, and it's good news to us if we ever feel left out, forgotten, or rejected.

Do you think the people criticizing Jesus thought it was good news? They were kind of like the older son in Jesus' story. When that son learned that his irresponsible younger brother was back and Dad was throwing a party, he got mad and refused to join in. "I did exactly what I was supposed to do! I didn't run off and waste Dad's money! Where's my party?"

He didn't know that he was lost, too, in a way. The father went out to find him, and when he did, he assured his older son that he mattered too. The party wasn't complete without him either. Everybody counts.

Discuss: Who gets overlooked or left out in your community? How can you help make sure they are included?

Discover: How many coins can you find in your house? Gather and count them, then decide what to do with them.

Do: Say something you love about each member of your family. Make sure each one knows they matter.

God, thank you for caring about each one of us so much, even if we wander away from you sometimes. Amen.

Faithful Steps

Read Matthew 6:25-34
Or "Don't Worry" (*Story Bible*, p. 342)

Do you ever feel worried? What sorts of things do you worry about? Maybe you get anxious when it storms outside, or you worry about grades or friendships. Anxiety can be crippling, and it affects even people with a strong faith in God.

Jesus' admonition not to worry can seem kind of out of touch. God feeds the birds and makes the flowers beautiful, sure, but that's a little different from humans needing to find food in a famine or afford groceries and clothes when money is tight. Jesus never had to deal with math tests or cyberbullying.

Despite his flowery language (no pun intended), Jesus' point was that God cares for you and knows what you are going through. The things that worry you are important, and they matter to God. In telling people not to worry, Jesus reminds us that worry can keep us paralyzed in fear and keep us from moving forward in faith.

When anxiety makes everything around you seem unknown, as if it is hidden in the dark, imagine God's love as a lantern you can carry with you. You may not be able to see everything that lies ahead, but you can see enough to take a step—and as you take each step, the light moves with you so that you can keep going.

Focus on taking the next faithful step or, as Jesus put it, "seek first the kingdom of God" (v. 33) and you will gain insight and confidence for your path, letting worry fall away.

Jesus said he is "the light of the world" (John 8:12) and also that we "are the light of the world" (Matt. 5:14). As we carry Jesus' light with us, we can shed light on other people's paths too, helping them to leave worry behind and take faithful steps together.

Discuss: What things do you worry about? What could be a next faithful step in facing those things?

Discover: Just before his teaching on worry, Jesus warned the people against having too many possessions. Read Matthew 6:19–21 and think about how owning too much stuff can lead to more worries and less faith.

Do: Make lanterns with glass jars and battery-operated tea lights. Soak empty jars in warm water to help remove food labels, and wrap a ribbon or pipe cleaner around the lip of the jar to make a handle. Practice walking in the dark with your lanterns illuminating just your next few steps.

Lord, help us not become stuck in worry but follow you one step at a time. Amen.

Seeing Jesus

Read Matthew 25:31-40
Or "Seeing Jesus" (*Story Bible*, p. 326)

Do you ever wish you had been alive to meet Jesus when he was walking on earth? It would have been amazing to see him heal people of diseases, turn water into wine, and walk on water. He was so caring with the people he met, always willing to stop and see what people needed—*really* needed, deep down. He probably gave really amazing hugs.

We can't hang out with Jesus in the flesh, like his friends did, but there are ways to see Jesus in our world today.

Jesus told his disciples how he would welcome people into the kingdom of God one day, saying, "You are blessed because I was hungry and you gave me food . . . I was a stranger and you welcomed me." The people would be confused, Jesus said. "When did we see you hungry and feed you?" they would ask. "When did we see you as a stranger and welcome you?" Jesus—the king in this story—would explain, "When you fed any hungry person, welcomed any stranger, visited any sick person or prisoner—you did it for me."

When you take care of people who need it, it's as if you are caring for Jesus. We love Jesus by loving people who are here on earth. You can see Jesus in them, and they can see Jesus in you—loving them as Jesus does. And when someone else cares for you, you can see Jesus in them too.

Spend some time this week seeing Jesus in those you meet. Who is hungry? Who is sick? Who needs help with clothes? Who is in prison of any kind? Who is a stranger who needs to be included? Look for Jesus in them, and you'll meet him face-to-face.

Discuss: Why were the people confused when Jesus said they had fed or visited him?

Discover: Look up the poem by Saint Teresa of Avila that begins, "Christ has no body but yours," and read it aloud.

Do: Regardless of how someone ended up there, prison is a lonely place to be. Contact the chaplain at a local prison to see what cards, letters, or small artwork can be sent.

God, help us see Jesus in everyone we meet and love others so well that they see Jesus in us. Amen.

A Different Sort of King

Read Luke 19:29-40
Or "Jesus Visits Jerusalem" (*Story Bible*, pp. 270-71)

You've probably seen a parade before or at least watched one in a movie or show. Have you ever been to a parade designed to celebrate just one person or a small group of people—like a local hero or winning sports team? Can you hear the excited screaming when the honoree comes by? Can you picture the hands waving wildly?

When Jesus approached the capital city of Jerusalem after a few years of teaching all over the towns and countryside, he asked his disciples to find a donkey for him to ride on. He usually walked everywhere, so it was a little strange for him to ride on a donkey. Even stranger was how the people lining the road into Jerusalem responded: they took off their cloaks and laid them on the path in front of Jesus. This is what people would do for a king returning home with their victorious army!

Some people even shouted out, "Blessed is the king who comes in the name of the Lord!" (v. 38). But Jesus wasn't a powerful ruler on a warhorse—he was a peaceful teacher on a donkey. He wasn't boasting about dominating an enemy army, he was preaching love for enemies. He was at the center of a royal-style parade but without the golden crowns and trumpets that would accompany a real king.

As Jesus had done so many times in his life, he turned people's expectations upside down—and it drove some people crazy. In this case, Jesus acting like a king (even in an ironic way) and people treating him like a king wasn't just confusing or strange. It was dangerous, because it could get Jesus' followers and all the Jews in Jerusalem in trouble with the real king.

> **Discuss:** In what ways is Jesus like a king? In what ways is he not?
>
> **Discover:** When we remember Jesus' arrival in Jerusalem at church, we call it Palm Sunday—but only one of the four Gospel versions of this story specifically mentions palm branches. Can you find which one it is?
>
> **Do:** Act out a scene of a triumphant king in a parade, and then act out the scene in today's story. What differences do you notice?

Lord, let us celebrate and honor Jesus every day. Help us remember that no king, leader, or celebrity on earth comes close to King Jesus. Amen.

Eat, Drink, and Remember

Read Luke 22:7-20
Or "A Passover Meal" (*Story Bible*, pp. 272-73)

Do you remember the story about when the Hebrew people were getting ready to flee slavery in Egypt? (See "Let My People Go" on pp. 38–39.) Moses told the people to roast a lamb and put some of the lamb's blood on their doors so that the plague of death would *pass over* their houses without hurting anyone, and after that, Pharaoh would set them free. Jewish people have celebrated the holiday of Passover for thousands of years, remembering the story of how God brought them out of slavery and into freedom.

Like many holiday celebrations, food is a central part of the tradition. On Passover, Jews eat roast lamb and other foods reminding them of the bitter hardships of slavery. They eat bread made without yeast or leavening, remembering how Moses told the people to make unleavened bread for their quick escape.

As a Jew, Jesus celebrated Passover each year. When he and his disciples arrived in Jerusalem, Jesus knew this might be the last holiday they would spend together, and he wanted them to remember it—and him—forever.

Like all the foods at the table, the bread and wine had special significance, and Jesus added even more.

"This is like my body, given for you," Jesus said. "Eat it and remember me." After dinner, Jesus did the same thing with the cup, saying "This is like my blood, making a new covenant with you."

The disciples must have been confused. Perhaps they thought, *How is Jesus giving his body for us? Why would we need to remember him? He's right here! And what is this new covenant?*

His disciples may not have understood, but they remembered. After Jesus died, they told others what he had said about his body and blood so that even now, thousands of years later, when followers of Jesus gather in churches or homes, they eat and drink together and remember Jesus.

Discuss: What do you think Jesus wanted his followers to remember about him?

Discover: Research how different churches practice this remembrance. Some may call it Communion, others the Lord's Supper, others the Eucharist, or perhaps the Great Thanksgiving.

Do: Buy some unleavened bread (called matzo) at the grocery store. Break it and taste it. Think about what it means to Jews remembering the first Passover and what it means for us remembering Jesus.

God, thank you for special foods and traditions that help us celebrate and remember. Amen.

Jesus Dies

Read Luke 23:13-49
Or "Jesus Dies" (*Story Bible*, p. 274)

The question "Why did Jesus get killed?" is a hard one. He preached that we should love God and love people—commandments God gave the people long before Jesus arrived! Who can disagree with love?

Still, we know Jesus made some people very uncomfortable. His message about the kingdom of God turning the world upside down—good news to those who were poor and outcast—didn't feel like good news to people for whom this world was working just fine.

A world in which the first become last and the last become first is a real challenge to the way we humans like to do things. We like to rank one another, to judge who is more worthy of acceptance, of praise, of money, and of power—and who isn't worthy. The systems we create, like governments and even religious organizations, often use those same criteria, keeping some people at the very top, some people at the bottom, and some people out altogether. The people on top like those systems pretty well, and they don't want anyone to mess things up for them.

Several groups of powerful people are involved in the story of Jesus' arrest, trial, and crucifixion. Jesus gets dragged back and

> **Crucifixion**, or nailing people to a wooden cross, was a way of putting to death the most despised criminals in the Roman Empire and other ancient empires.

forth between the religious leaders and the Roman officials, none of whom like him very much because they see him as a threat to their orderly system.

It wasn't fair or right. Jesus didn't deserve to die. But he didn't fight it. He didn't call down angels from heaven to rescue him. He wanted people to see what sinful human power does and how God's power works differently.

Where human powers fear, condemn, torture, and kill, Jesus radiated peace and love to his dying breath. To those hurting him, he offered forgiveness, and to the terrified man on the cross beside his, he offered comfort.

When Jesus died, it may have seemed like the powerful people won, but it wasn't the end of the story.

Discuss: How would you have felt if you were one of Jesus' followers, seeing Jesus arrested and killed?

Discover: Visit the Innocence Project and the Equal Justice Initiative online to learn about people today who are accused falsely and punished excessively.

Do: Make a list of people and groups who have the most power in our world today and of those who have the least.

God, we know that the world is not the way you want it to be. Help us remember that love wins in the end, even when things are sad and scary. Amen.

Jesus Lives

Read Luke 24:1-12
Or "Women at the Tomb" (*Story Bible*, pp. 276-77)

Death feels like the most final thing in the world, doesn't it? When someone dies, we mourn that we can never hold their hand again, never have a conversation again, never do the things we enjoyed doing together again. We may pick up the phone to call or text them and then remember that they're not able to answer anymore.

Jesus' friends were feeling that finality after his death. They would never get to talk with him again, never hear his stories, or share a meal with him ever again. Some of the women who were closest to Jesus went to his tomb early the day after the Sabbath, expecting to find his dead body in the tomb, right where they'd seen it laid. Why would they expect anything different?

And yet the tomb was empty! "He is not here. He has risen!" the mysterious, glowing figures said.

The women had seen Jesus do so many amazing things—things no one else could do. But to rise from the dead? That was impossible!

They should have known that with Jesus, things are not always what they seem. It may seem that a child born in a humble manger is not very important, but he was. It may seem that some people don't matter, but they do. It may seem that powerful people can put an innocent man to death and silence his message forever, but they couldn't.

It may seem like death has the final word, but God's love is more powerful than even death. That's what Jesus' resurrection is all about.

> **Resurrection** means coming back to life after one has died.

There are many sad things in the world. Friendships end. Disasters happen. People and pets pass away. But the love and life that is in Jesus goes on forever.

Discuss: What does it mean to you that Jesus conquered death and came back to life?

Discover: The men in dazzling clothes said, "Remember how he told you he would rise again?" Read Luke 9:18–24 to see how.

Do: Make "resurrection rolls" with packaged dough, marshmallows, butter, and cinnamon sugar. Find instructions online to create these treats that go into the oven full and come out as empty tombs.

Hallelujah, Lord! Jesus is risen! Thank you for your powerful love that lives forever. Amen.

Faith and Doubt

Read John 20:19-31
Or "Thomas Wants to See" (*Story Bible*, p. 278)

Have you ever had a nickname that you hated or had someone tease you using a name that unfortunately caught on?

One of the twelve disciples, Thomas, was understandably skeptical when the others told him that Jesus had risen from the dead. "Unless I see it for myself, I won't believe it!" he said. And for that, he was labeled "Doubting Thomas" by countless Christians throughout history.

It's not exactly fair to shame Thomas for not believing something that was, frankly, unbelievable! Jesus—who had been killed and buried—had just appeared to the other disciples, showing up in a room behind a locked door, no less. Thomas just happened to not be there at the time.

> **Doubt** means being unsure about something, wanting more information.

Maybe he'd volunteered to go get food for everyone. The others probably wouldn't have believed it either if they hadn't seen it with their own eyes.

They all wanted to see Jesus for themselves because they loved him. Asking questions and wanting to know more is a sign you care.

Imagine telling someone about something cool you saw or did. If they respond, "Oh, that's nice," they might believe you, but they don't really care. If they respond, "Really? Let me see!" they might be unsure, but you can tell they care.

Jesus appeared to the disciples again a week later, and this time, Thomas was there. Jesus spoke to Thomas directly and let him touch his wounds. "It's really me, Thomas!" you can imagine him saying. Jesus was happy to reassure his friend. Jesus welcomes the questions and feelings we have. Jesus also made sure to say that people don't have to have seen him to believe in him—a nod to all those followers who would come later, like us.

Doubt is not the opposite of faith but an important part of it. Faith and doubt go hand in hand because we care enough about God to want to know more. Many things about God are a mystery. Faithful followers have many questions, and they keep seeking answers their whole lives.

Discuss: What do you think Jesus' resurrected body was like? Remember that no one knows for sure, and that's OK!

Discover: Find out where Thomas is said to have traveled and started a church.

Do: Write down a list of questions you have about God.

God, you are bigger and more amazing than we can understand. Bless our questions and help us know you more every day. Amen.

Speaking in the Spirit

Read Acts 2:1-41
Or "Pentecost" (*Story Bible*, pp. 288-89)

Jesus spent forty days on earth after his resurrection before rising up to heaven. He promised not to leave his followers alone, though. God's Holy Spirit would come to them and empower them to continue Jesus' work on earth.

Ten days later—fifty days after Easter—Jesus' disciples were all gathered together celebrating the Jewish holiday of Pentecost. Pentecost celebrates the day God gave Moses the Ten Commandments. The disciples might not have felt much like celebrating, without their friend and teacher there with them, but maybe they read the story from Exodus and remembered how God spoke through mighty thunder and appeared to Moses in fire. How lucky they had been to hear God speak through Jesus!

Suddenly a powerful wind blew through the house and little flames settled over each person. Was this the Holy Spirit? Was God giving them commandments as God had done with Moses? They opened their mouths to speak, and words came out that they did not recognize! Outside the house, Jews who had come to Jerusalem from many lands for the holiday heard the ruckus and were surprised to hear these men speaking the languages of their homelands. "How is this possible?" they said.

The Holy Spirit had empowered them, just as Jesus had said, to reach many different people with his message. That day, it was by speaking other languages. As time went on, God's Spirit would do other amazing things through them as they traveled far and wide to preach the good news of Jesus. From that small band of followers who had known Jesus personally, the group that would come to be known as Christians grew and grew.

Even today, the Holy Spirit still moves in people, helping us show the world what we've learned from Jesus. When you see someone in pain and feel that nudge in your heart to reach out and help—that's the Holy Spirit, empowering you to love like Jesus.

> **Discuss:** Why do you think the Holy Spirit made the disciples speak in different languages?

> **Discover:** How many languages are there in the world? Do you think people worship God in every language there is?

> **Do:** Pentecost is sometimes called the birthday of the church. Find a sweet treat, put a candle in it, and sing "Happy Birthday" to the movement of Jesus' followers that is more than two thousand years old!

Lord, thank you for the gift of your Holy Spirit and for the many followers who keep the message of Jesus alive. Amen.

Enough for Everyone

Read Acts 2:42-47; 4:32-35
Or "Living Together" (*Story Bible*, pp. 290-91)

What does it mean to be a community? A group of people who live near each other, who work or go to school together? How can a community make life good for everyone? How should the community take care of people who do not have enough money or food?

The community of Jesus' followers in Jerusalem tried to live in the way they thought Jesus would want them to. They ate together and worshiped God together. They worked together to make sure that everyone had food, shelter, clothing, and whatever else they needed so that no one was poor. They sold things they didn't really need—even houses and land—and pooled their money together so that everyone would have enough of what they needed.

We don't know how long they were able to live like this, because the church kept growing and it got harder to manage things with more people. There were some complications—some people lied and tried to keep some secret money for themselves, even though they'd agreed to give it all to the group. You can imagine it might be hard to trust leaders to be fair with the communal money, especially if the group had gotten so big that you didn't know the leaders very well.

Throughout history, some small communities have chosen to live like the early Jerusalem church did, pooling their resources and taking care of everyone's needs. Most of us don't live like that today, but remembering the story of how the first

Christians lived can still help us think about how to live faithfully as followers of Jesus. How can we help make life good for everyone? How can our community take care of people who do not have enough money or food? How can our money help other people have enough of what they need?

Our communities may be very different from the first church, but the goal of living as Jesus wants is the same.

Discuss: Would you want to live in a community like the Jerusalem church? Why or why not?

Discover: Research intentional communities that exist today. What are some characteristics of these communities?

Do: Host a few other families for a potluck meal and talk about what it would mean to be in community with one another.

Lord, show us how to help our communities become places where everyone has enough. Amen.

From Persecutor to Preacher

Read Acts 8:1-3; 9:1-19
Or "Saul's Change of Heart" (*Story Bible*, pp. 296-97)

In the early years of the church, Christians were still part of the Jewish faith, like Jesus had been. Non-Jews who heard about Jesus and wanted to follow him became Jews—Jews who followed Jesus. One Jewish man named Saul was not happy that so many Jews were following Jesus. He thought that people who were following Jesus needed to be arrested or even killed. He barged into people's houses and dragged them off to prison.

Imagine being a Christian in that time and hearing that Saul was coming to your town. What would you do? Go into hiding until he went away? You probably would not want to seek him out and help him. Ananias sure didn't want to do that, even when Jesus appeared in a vision and asked him to.

Ananias certainly didn't expect Saul to have a radical change of heart. But Jesus had appeared to Saul as well, blinding him with a bright light and calling him out for persecuting Jesus' followers. Jesus told Ananias to find Saul and restore his sight. Saul would be transformed from a persecutor of Christians to a preacher of Jesus Christ's gospel!

> To **persecute** someone means to harass or cause someone to suffer because of their beliefs, origin, or other personal characteristics.

In particular, Jesus chose Saul to take his message to people who were not Jewish, who the Jewish people called Gentiles.

Saul spent the rest of his life traveling around, starting churches, and helping them work through the challenges that came from Jews and non-Jews trying to follow Jesus together. He even said that non-Jews didn't have to become Jewish to be Christian. No matter what religion you were born into or what language you spoke, you could be part of the church.

Much of the New Testament is made up of letters written by Saul, who is more often called Paul. He may have started out as a bad guy in the story, but Jesus can change anybody's heart and use anybody to do good in the world.

> **Discuss:** How do you think Saul felt, having his heart changed so dramatically by Jesus?
>
> **Discover:** Where are people today being persecuted for their religion?
>
> **Do:** Make up your own story about a bad guy being transformed into a good guy.

God, change our hearts when they need to be changed, and keep our minds open to know others can change too. Amen.

Part of the Body

Read 1 Corinthians 12:12-31
Or "One Church" (*Story Bible*, pp. 306-7)

Imagine people two thousand years from now reading the text messages you send your friends. Would they be able to tell when you were being sarcastic or what certain slang terms meant? Those messages might be a little confusing to people in the distant future, but there might also be nuggets of wisdom that even forty-first-century people could appreciate: Like when your friend thanks you for listening and you say, "That's what friends are for."

This is kind of what it's like reading the letters from Paul and other early church leaders that are included in the Bible. We're reading somebody else's mail, so not everything applies to us, and some of it just sounds a little weird. But some parts offer valuable teachings about how to follow Jesus and how to get along in a community.

Paul wrote long letters to the communities of Christians he'd helped start in cities all around the Mediterranean Sea, offering encouragement and guidance for the problems the new churches were having. The church in Corinth, a city in Greece, was apparently struggling with a lot of debates, including about what the most important jobs in the church were.

Paul told them that every person, every gift they bring, every task they do is essential to the community. Preaching isn't better than teaching, and healing isn't more important than serving food. The church is like a human body, Paul said. All the body parts matter, from the head to the feet and the ears to the fingers! The parts are different sizes and do different things, but they are all essential, just like every person in the group.

We tend to rank these things, with apostles (like Paul) at the top, but that doesn't mean those people should be given greater respect. In the way of Jesus, Paul reminds them, those that the world regards as small and unimportant should be treated as the most valuable.

> **Discuss:** What gifts do you have that you use to serve God? Have you ever felt that your gift isn't as important as someone else's?
>
> **Discover:** Turn to your Bible's table of contents. How many letters are included in the Bible? To how many different churches or individuals were those letters sent?
>
> **Do:** Write an actual paper letter to a relative or friend who lives far away. What news will you share with them?

God, help us remember that we all have different and valuable gifts to share with the world. Thank you for the ways in which we can all work together. Amen.

All Cheering for You

Read Hebrews 11:23-12:2
Or "You Can Do It!" (*Story Bible*, pp. 312-13)

Do you ever pull out old photos and remember the people who came before you? You see the smiles of grandparents and other older relatives, including many who maybe aren't alive anymore. Maybe there's an old school photo with a teacher you loved but haven't seen in years. Even pictures of yourself from when you were younger can remind you how much you've grown and changed in the time since.

One of the final letters included in the Bible uses this kind of nostalgia to encourage Christians who are having a really hard time. Even though Saul (Paul) had stopped persecuting Christians, many others started as more and more churches were founded and Christians became a growing but unpopular minority in the Roman Empire. Many people were discriminated against, arrested, and even put to death.

The Christians receiving this letter were scared and discouraged, wondering how they could go on as faithful followers of Jesus when everything seemed to be against them. So the writer of Hebrews reminded them of the faithful people who had come before them.

Remember how Moses gave up his princely status and stood up to Pharaoh to free his people?

Remember how Rahab bravely hid the Hebrew spies and escaped Jericho before it fell?

Remember Samuel and the other prophets who spoke hard truths to powerful people?

Who else do you remember reading about? There have been so many people playing important roles in God's story, inspiring all the people who came after them. We can imagine their faces looking down on us from heaven like "so great a cloud of witnesses" (12:1), as the letter writer put it.

When you are struggling and feel as if you can't keep going, imagine you're running an important race. You're not running alone, but as part of a relay in which the people who've come before have passed the baton to you. They're all cheering for you as you run your part of the race. You look forward and see Jesus, who taught you how to run—how to live—and eventually you'll see the people to whom you'll pass the baton. They'll be looking to you, and you'll cheer them on too.

Discuss: Who do you picture cheering you on when you're having a tough time?

Discover: Call an older relative or an older person at church and ask them who most inspired them in their faith.

Do: Make a list together of people who have inspired you to live faithfully so that you can look at it when you need encouragement. Start each line with, "Remember [*person's name*], who . . ."

God, thank you for all the people in the Bible, in history, and in our own lives who have shown us how to follow you. Amen.

www.ingramcontent.com/pod-product-compliance
Lightning Source LLC
Chambersburg PA
CBHW072012290426
44109CB00018B/2210